INNER CHILD RECOVERY WORK WITH RADICAL SELF COMPASSION

SELF-CONTROL PRACTICES AND EMOTIONAL
INTELLIGENCE; FROM CONFLICT TO RESOLUTION
FOR BETTER RELATIONSHIPS

DON BARLOW

A ROADTOTRANQUILITY™ BOOK

CONTENTS

Part II
THE INNER CHILD WORK TOWARDS
BETTER RELATIONSHIP WITH SELF
AND OTHERS

Part III
TIPS FOR STAYING ON TOP OF
YOUR GAME

NO MORE

START SAYING NO
LEARN TO SAY NO WITHOUT
EXPLAINING YOURSELF

DON BARLOW

Before we get into the book, let me offer you a free mini-book. Scan QR code to claim your FREE
People-Pleasing No More mini-book!

INTRODUCTION

Remember when you were a child, that you never worried about tomorrow or beyond? Instead, you were always in the present moment, carefree, exploring new things and having fun. You were not afraid to express yourself and tell someone exactly how you felt. Somewhere along the line, you grew up and became a responsible adult. Part of that freshness and honesty was lost. The more you learned, the more you began to overthink things to the point that you hesitated to take chances. It became more difficult to let yourself go or have fun because those things began to seem inappropriate or even unsafe to you.

When you are emotionally overwhelmed, you tend to regress and subconsciously fall into a habitual pattern of self-defeating thoughts and actions that pull you down. This repeatedly happens every time you feel overloaded, stressed, challenged, or conflicted. What you don't realize is that there is a wounded child inside you. It's from this child that your present anger, fear, anxiety, and insecurities come. Whatever you have become today is a result of this inner child within you trying to handle your adult issues. You're trying to find this childhood self. You want to eventually acknowledge it, so you can reconcile your current adult self with that wounded inner child. Otherwise, you will continue to self-sabotage yourself with self-defeating patterns that you seem to have no control over.

When it comes to your inner child, your personality type is joyous, cheerful, emotional, excited, feeling, playful, and giddy. Your energy level, as well as your mood, determines your condition. You will experience a period of indifference, as your exterior living condition changes. Similar to your inner child, your outer child generally is cheerful, joyful, and delightfully adventurous. The bottom portion of the diaphragm "Three Selves" is an elaborate model of the human psyche. A group of experts in psychology have asserted that the inner child is a human being's true infantile nature. It includes all of your education and life experiences that are in one place before the onset of puberty. The inner child represents a self-reliant persona subordinate entity, who is under your conscious control.

How to Discover Your Inner Child

By learning how to go inward and discover your inner child, you will have a contented and balanced life. To learn more about your inner child, you can do the following:

Do not restrict your actions - you need to constantly compare how impulsive you are today, with how impulsive you were when you were a child. Instead of disregarding your inner voice, give your full attention to it. You should also adjust your present timetable to make room for this new schedule.

Allow yourself to be imaginative – not only in what you do but also in how you think. You must also encourage your imagination and let your ideas fly with different creative exercises.

Maintain a positive mental attitude - make time to laugh and smile. It doesn't mean that you have to go around grinning all the time. However, you can certainly surround yourself with things that will make your life more fascinating and thrilling. You can either interact with youngsters or you can play games on your own. While you are exercising, put on your favorite music or watch funny videos.

Use your senses - they will activate your entire world. They will make the world seem brighter. Take time to notice the aroma and visual qualities of your surrounding environment. You also need to appreciate the food, textiles, and everything else. Discovering your inner child can be as simple as following these few steps. Checking up with your inner child helps you repair old traumas.

How to Heal Your Inner Child

The emotional scars you bear from your childhood may deepen over time. You will often develop emotional vulnerabilities and behave as a dysfunctional adult. Therefore, you have to recreate history. If you don't, you will never discover genuine well-being, and be happy in your own life. Treatment of the inner child, on the other hand, is not simple or quick. Here are the several actions you can take to mend your shattered inner child to serve as a guide:

Earn Your Inner Child's Trust -You must cultivate trust in order to repair your wounded inner child. It implies that your inner child must have faith in you. Your inner child should be aware that you're there to look after it and safeguard it.

Sustain Its Excruciating Pains -You're like a scared child. You must assist your inner child in fighting and moving on. Make an effort to learn to accept and understand your inner child's grief; embracing the pains of your inner child will get you one step ahead of the game. This is excellent recuperation.

Let Go of Your Anger -It is natural to be angry. We all get upset and unhappy about things, but that doesn't mean you have to let yourself be furious all the time. You have an opportunity to repair your inner child, if you forgive. Forgiveness takes a lot of love and concern for others.

Defend Against Loneliness - This is another kind of treatment for your shattered inner child. Make sure your inner child is happy, accepts itself as it is, and realizes its genuine self. You must assist it in feeling free of guilt and humiliation.

You have the opportunity to embrace a new and exciting life, by following these simple guidelines on how to restore your inner child. Don't underestimate your inner child's power. Are you ready to bring your inner child back to life? Then begin treating it, and you will see that it has a positive impact on your life.

PART I

LOVING THE INNER CHILD

1

MEET THE SWEET, INNER CHILD

Focus: Why don't we introduce ourselves to a person we'd almost forgotten about - our own inner child?

As people grow older, their perception of the world naturally changes due to their experiences in life. Failures, successes, trials, and pleasures shape their mind. It is easy to get lost in adulthood - bills to pay, employers to obey, clients to chase, spouses to please, and children to raise. The pressures of the world start to weigh down on people, so they begin looking for an escape…even for just a little while. Some book an expensive vacation somewhere, some have an affair, and others just up and leave.

What many don't actually know is that they have yet to reclaim their inner child, the purest part of their mind that sees the world through an innocent's eyes. Your inner child is the childlike aspect of yourself, the version that used to exist before puberty took hold of you.

Whenever you reminisce on your childhood memories, you are subconsciously attempting to reawaken your inner child. However, this usually lasts only for a moment. Reality will begin to sink in. There are also individuals whose childhood experiences were not so good, maybe even traumatic. That is why they tend to repress all that was in the past. However, when the time is right, you would like to tap into that lost corner of your mind where your inner child awaits you.

In the realm of Psychology, the inner child is one of the "Three Selves" of the human psyche. The inner child, even before the bruises of reality, is joyful, emotional, playful, curious, adventurous, loving, and friendly. Its thoughts revolve around the simple pleasures in life - the smell of freshly cut grass, the coolness of a breeze, and the sound of waves lapping on the seashore. Awakening the Inner Child inside of you will change how you view the world and how you react to everything that life throws at you.

STEPS TO DISCOVERING YOUR INNER CHILD

Each person's inner child is unique, so take your time in awakening the long, lost childlike aspect of your mind because it can be challenging for some people.

Choose a particular moment in your life when your worries are at a minimum. It can be on a weekend or even just a free afternoon. This moment will be the opportunity for you to embark on a journey to discovering your inner child. You do not have to follow all of these steps, nor follow them in a linear manner.

Open up Mementos. In order to discover your inner child, you can browse through old photographs of yourself when you were still young. If you used to write journals, open them up and read what your thoughts were when you were in elementary school. You can also go up to the attic to become reacquainted with your old toys.

These mementos can bring back a flood of old memories, so do your best to maintain an open mind. Focus on the happy moments in your childhood, then close your eyes and do your best to recall how you used to view the world during those times. These childlike thoughts can help you tap into the subconscious and hopefully discover your inner child.

Visit your Favorite Childhood Spots. If you have the time, visit the old places that were filled with happy memories of your childhood. It can be your kindergarten or elementary school, the playground next to your worship place, your old bedroom, or even the tree where you used to climb.

Some of these places have likely changed, but when you are there, you can still invoke the memories attached to these places and how you, as a child, used to feel and think. The monkey bars were more than just steel and paint; this was your jungle. The slide wasn't just a sheet of metal but was the edge of the world. Hold on to these thoughts, for these are glimpses of your inner child.

Watch TV shows and Movies from your Childhood. When you were a child, you enjoyed the wonders that television showed you. It was like a magical box filled with super-heroes, magical stories, and scary tales. These shows and movies were more than just a distraction. They opened up new doors to your imagination, by introducing new concepts into your schema.

Now, as an adult, you might think that these old TV shows are silly, or these movies have such unrealistic plots that you would rather do something more productive. However, give them a chance to delight you once more. Let go of your modern-day adulthood worries, and just enjoy the romance, action, and comedy that these childhood shows have. Remember when you wanted to become a Power Ranger and practiced your "fighting skills" with your friends? Or when you listened to "Puff the Magic Dragon" and you wished with all your might that he could take you to his magical world as well? Recall how you reveled in these shows as a child and don't let those feelings go.

Create an "Inner Child" Map. Adults have a different way of viewing things compared to a child. This activity is a bridge between how you think now as an adult and how your inner child thinks. Adults usually prefer to create organizers or charts to plan or understand something. This time you will be creating an organizer, more specifically called a semantic map, that can help you discover your inner child.

To create an "inner child" map, you can get a picture of yourself as a child, probably around the age of seven or eight. If you do not have any pictures, then you can simply draw yourself when you were that age. Place the picture or the drawing at the center of a piece of paper, with enough room for scribbles all around it. Then, begin recalling as much as you can all of the phrases or words that you associate with this child version of you. Brainstorm everything, such as your favorite color back then, the gifts that you wanted for holidays, your nickname, your favorite movie, the book that you kept reading over and over again with a flashlight under your blanket, an imaginary friend, or the silly urban legends that you used to believe in. Once you have finished your "inner child map," you are much closer to discovering it, if you haven't already.

Fulfil One Wish from Your Inner Child. As a child, you probably wanted a lot of things that you couldn't have because your parents wouldn't allow you or were unable to afford them. You wanted to grow up fast to get whatever you wanted: stay up late and watch TV, buy that seemingly expensive action figure or stuffed animal, or go to Disney World. Now that you are all grown up, you have probably forgotten these childlike whims because you are so preoccupied with the demands of work and other responsibilities.

You have every opportunity to grant this request and make the child in you ecstatic. Buy that expensive toy, watch those old cartoons until one o'clock in the morning, or go ahead and visit Disney World. Don't do it because you feel the need to satisfy, but because you wanted to for so long but never did.

Write a Letter to Your Inner Child. Recalling old memories of your childhood can awaken your inner child from sleep. As your emotions are stirred by the memories, you can compose a message to your inner child and hope for it to come back. This might sound like a crazy idea to some. However, it can really help you feel more relaxed and at peace.

Your style in composing the letter should be as if you are really talking to a child. Add drawings and scribbles, if you wish. Include recollections from your memories, such as writing something like: "Remember the time when you poked that old crab in the creek and it got so angry you feared it would cut your toes off?" You can also say how you feel now as an adult about the good and bad experiences that your child-self went through. It could be: "I really felt mad at Auntie Tracy when she said that your drawing looked awful; it was a bad thing to say to a kid." You can also tell your inner child about all the things that you went through in puberty, young adulthood and adulthood, such as your accomplishments and silly mistakes. Lastly, ask for your inner child to come back into your life and help you find yourself again.

FINDING YOUR TRUE SELF WITH THE HELP OF YOUR INNER CHILD

Hopefully, your journey to discovering your inner child was an enriching experience. Tears, laughter and frustrations are normal emotions that come with recalling your childhood and everything that is attached to it. We may have drifted from our old selves, but our roots can never be changed. By discovering your inner child, you are going back to those roots and really reflecting upon yourself and what you want out of life.

Now that you have rekindled your relationship with your inner child, you can begin to take steps to finding your true self. There are several suggestions on how you can go about it below. You are also free to choose one which you are most comfortable with. You may use a pen and paper to note down all of the things that come into your mind as you encounter each detail that your inner child can share with you.

"When I grow up I want to be..." What was your answer to this question when your teacher asked you? Did you say that you wanted to be a pilot like your grandfather, a veterinarian like your aunt, a fireman like good old dad or an astronaut you saw on TV? Your inner child will answer anything its heart desires because it believes that anything is possible. Your adult self might say it is virtually impossible now, but is it really true?

When we were still children, we could always answer whatever we wanted about when we grow up because our future was way ahead of us. Anything could happen. As we got older, many factors came into play - money problems, economic depression, low demand or high supply. We, therefore, chose to follow the path that society pointed for us, instead of what our inner child really, truly wanted.

While this doesn't necessarily mean you need to follow the path your inner child wanted you to all those years ago, when it answered the question. It is the reason behind why your child-self chose that answer, that may lead you to understand more about your true self. For example, why did you want to become a veterinarian? It may be because you want to help sick animals. It means that deep inside, you are a kind-hearted person who is full of compassion. Why did you say you wanted to become a fireman? Is it because you admired your father for saving lives while risking his own? Your true self must want very much to help others in need. You can answer that longing by joining an outreach program. If your inner child says that you want to be the richest person in the world, it's possible that you want to own a business that will allow you to earn a lot of money and at the same time provide jobs for many people.

Go ahead and let your inner child answer this question once more. Open your mind and do not let the world's conventions influence its voice.

"**My hopes and dreams...**" Viewing the world through a child's innocent eyes will enable you to see things from a fresh perspective. This can lead you to discovering your true hopes and dreams that are untainted by society. What did you wish for, when you were still a child? Try to recall what you wanted in your life back then. Think of how simple things were, before you found out about the tougher side of life. All you ever wanted was to play with your friends, have your mom tell you stories before you go to bed or make your dad swing you up onto his shoulders so that you could pretend to be the tallest kid on the block. When it all comes down to it, all you ever really hoped for and dreamed about was to be happy and loved.

Money and power have consumed so many adults that they have forgotten what their true hopes and dreams are. They begin to chase these so-called symbols of prosperity. However, in the process, they lose the very thing that inspired them to work so hard. That is why it is healthy to be reminded by your inner child of what truly matters in life. That is happiness and love.

What will make you happy? Financial security can make you feel happy when you really stop to think about it. However, the happiness of being with good company is just as important, if not more so. Your inner child will want you to play, talk about silly things, laugh and just have good, clean fun. Happiness can be found in feeling the sand between your toes, chatting with an old friend, and enjoying a hot cup of chocolate indoors while it's raining. If you appreciate all of the little things that made you very happy as a child, you will realize that it's all you ever hoped for.

What will make you feel loved? The inner child wants to love and be loved. It enjoys the feeling of embrace, a kiss on the cheek and actually saying "I love you." It also likes to stretch out its arms and say, "this big." Share your love with others. Embrace your family and tell the person you admire that you love them without expecting anything in return. If you think that no one loves you, then you have yet to meet man's best friend. That is a dog to give you loyalty and unconditional love, no matter who you are.

The simplicity of the inner child's hopes and dreams can inspire your adult self to strive for better things in life. Don't worry too much about what society thinks or that you are not rich enough or good-looking enough. As long as you have fulfilled your hopes and dreams of happiness and love, then nothing else really matters.

"How I truly feel..." As we continued to mature, we learned to put on different masks or facades. We have learned to hide how we honestly feel, in order to avoid unpleasant encounters in life, such as pain, bitterness, rejection and disappointment. While these defense mechanisms do serve a healthy purpose to protect ourselves, we sometimes become detached from our true selves because of this fear. Sometimes these true feelings get bottled up and stowed away in some corner inside of our minds, until they grow to become so big that we eventually burst and crack. The inner child can help you recover from this habit of holding it all in, by letting you accept how you truly feel. Keep in mind that accepting your true feelings is not necessarily the same as taking action.

For instance, many individuals have cheated on their partner because they hide their feelings of having "fallen out of love." They had to wait until they were tempted, before they listened to their inner child. It led to them inflicting pain and sorrow upon another. This would have been avoided, if the person had acknowledged how they felt about their partner beforehand. The inner child can point out these true feelings and then enable the adult side to handle the situation maturely.

On a lighter note, letting your inner child recognize how you truly feel can point you to even better things in life. For example, if you are stuck in a job that you do not like, your adult side might force you to stay there because you need it to pay the bills. However, the inner child knows better and is telling you that you do hate this job and you do feel that you are wasting your life on something that doesn't matter at all to you. By recognizing these true feelings, you can actually go about making plans for a more fulfilling career.

Let your inner child whisper your true feelings about something, instead of masking it or hiding it away. By doing so, your true self will be revealed.

"What I can create..." While we were kids, our creativity and imagination soared. The sandbox became a kingdom and the sand became a castle. Cardboard boxes became spaceships or time machines. Furniture became bodies of land, while the carpet became a sea of hot lava. The inner child is naturally creative and imaginative. It can open up the world of wonderment, the door to which has remained closed for so long.

By listening to your inner child, you will be able to envision and create things and think outside the box. The possibilities become endless and the creative juices will overflow. Your adult self will greatly benefit from the imaginative nature of your inner child. Even the great artist Pablo Picasso once said, "Every child is an artist. The problem is how to remain an artist once he grows up."

Chapter Summary

Since this chapter was the first in the book, we looked at an introduction to the person referred to as your inner child.

We, therefore, learned the following:

- Steps to Discovering Your Inner Child
- Open up Mementos
- Visit your Favorite Childhood Spots
- Watch TV shows and Movies from your Childhood
- Create an "Inner Child" Map
- Fulfil One Wish from Your Inner Child

- Write a Letter to Your Inner Child
- Finding Your True Self with the Help of Your Inner Child
- When I grow up, I want to be…
- My hopes and dreams
- How I truly feel
- What I can create

In the next chapter, you will learn A Careful but Thorough Diagnosis of Your Inner Child.

2

A CAREFUL BUT THOROUGH
DIAGNOSIS

Focus: How to know for sure whether your inner child is hurt or not.

Can we help having an injured, or worse still, dead inner child? Given that we all pass through life's developmental stages from childhood to adulthood, this is almost impossible. As we grow up, we are forced by time and nature to witness life-changing events and undergo impactful experiences, which may be positive or otherwise. Like the shoe prints on a wet, muddy path, these experiences leave us with significant and indelible influences that shape our growth process over time. In the process, we gradually lose touch with our inner child. Yet, this may be described as a rather simple natural change, like the passing of time, where we drift away from the inner child personality. This is a phenomenon that we cannot help. In the same vein, the inner child could be gravely wounded via specific untoward situations that occur to us by some external unnatural factors which are equally, if not more, dangerous. Examples of such situations include maltreatment, bullying, harassment of any sort, rape, repression, starvation, excessive pampering, accidents, neglect, and so on. By virtue of these circumstances, especially if they occur during one's formative period, an individual's inner child may be grossly injured. It's very likely that no individual ever enjoys a completely hitch-free ride from childhood to adulthood. Therefore, we are all victims of a wounded inner child, but to various degrees.

Against this background, it becomes a core necessity for every human alive to heal and recover their inner child. The problem with this, however, is that there are many people worldwide who cannot tell when their inner child has been injured, or which aspects of it are affected. In the recovery process, you must be able to do this. At this point, it is necessary to address this common deficiency through the use of the following signs. The clues provided here are not definitive on their own and do not apply to every individual. However, they will serve as a guide through your own inner child discovery.

HIDING YOUR TRUE FEELINGS

"I cannot understand what you do not say."

— KATE MCGAHAN

This is one of the most obvious signs exhibited by individuals with a wounded inner child. Given that they have been hurt, abused, repressed, bullied, or harassed, they conceal their feelings and continue to bear the hurt. They also believe that they are alone in it. This is wrong! As a result, they prefer to keep their true feelings bottled up. That explains why they almost never share their pain with others. They don't recognize that divulging one's hurt to others is a major step in the healing process. Most victims grow up with this inner child attitude and sometimes unfairly expect their partners to understand them as they are. Unfortunately, not everyone can understand their unspoken words. When they are pushed to it, victims of a wounded inner child will prefer to suppress their hurt and hide their true feelings. This situation permeates all aspects of their life, including family and work. Apart from getting hurt the most, they often give the wrong impression to others.

FAILURE TO TRUST OR BELIEVE IN OTHERS

"We are not strangers. It's a lack of trust that keeps us separated".

— MICHAEL R. FRENCH

It is logical to expect that one of the most common consequences of an injured inner child is lack of trust. Most of the events that occur during childhood leading to a wounded inner child are caused by close relations with people who we believe in: parents, siblings, friends, teachers, etc. The things they do to hurt us in our early years, dampens our trust in people. We begin to trust less and doubt more. When this is unchecked, we grow up with the mindset that no one can be trusted. This mindset often leads to more serious situations, such as depression and severe negativity. It makes it difficult for victims to share their problems with others. Individuals with trust problems keep their problems to themselves.

HIDING OR OVERBLOWING YOUR EGO

"Don't talk about yourself; it will be done when you leave."

— WILSON MIZNER

Ego describes your personal identity and sense of self-esteem. Ego usually isn't dangerous to your personality or your relationship with others. However, a very small ego or an overblown one may be a problem, which can be traced to your childhood experiences. When you think too little of yourself and find yourself constantly apologizing for other people's actions, it is possible that your pride has been affected by a childhood experience. These people are vulnerable to further abuse as adults. Excessive ego is also a product of an injured inner child. Individuals with the eternal child archetype, who were raised with the orientation that the world revolves around them, often fall into this category. They grow up to become disliked by others around them because they are often haughty, bossy, and disrespectful.

INSECURITY

"Most bad behavior comes from insecurity."

— DEBRA WINGER

Do you often feel insecure around people? You should check your inner child. People who grew up in homes with domestic violence or who suffered childhood abuse often carry insecurity into their adult life. They become unsure of their abilities because they have been told that they are worthless. They also fear others and would rather remain alone. However, when they are with other people, they hide their insecurities in haughtiness and jealousy. Insecurity may also result from the feeling of being completely useless. While growing up, many children are put under the pressure of comparison by their parents or significant others. You have most probably heard parents say statements such as *'Taylor already solves difficult sums, and you can't do anything!' or 'Abby now babysits her twin siblings. All you do is play around.'* Even when these comparisons are not clearly spelled out, they still do mental damage to the child. The victims see themselves as inferior to those who they are compared to.

LOSS OF CONFIDENCE IN ONESELF AND ONE'S ABILITIES

"It took me a long time not to judge myself through someone else's eyes."

— SALLY FIELD

Closely related to insecurity is lack of confidence. This is another sign of a wounded inner child. Negative comments and unfair comparisons by parents about their children do more than discourage them. These children lose their intrinsic motivation and become extremely dependent on assessments from others. They grow up to become dependent adults. It is difficult for them to make decisions on their own. They also rely too heavily on others approval of their actions. They feel inadequate and incapable. As a result, they find it difficult to accept that they are independently capable of achieving life's goals. They become too dependent on others and are prone to exploitation.

EXCESSIVE WORRY

"Worry does not empty tomorrow of its sorrow; it empties today of its strength."

— CORRIE TEN BOOM

For individuals with childhoods that had many catastrophic events, they have lost their joy about life. They hold the pessimistic belief that happiness is only temporary and will soon be replaced by gloominess. They live their lives in perpetual fear that the next moment will only be worse. As a result, they lose their ability to deal with challenges that they experience in life. Although there are times when their lives appear to be going well, they fear that tragedy is just around the corner. They are plagued by worry that has long been stamped on their inner child by adverse events from their childhood. As a result, they feel completely powerless to fight it. This individual will be resigned to the feeling that what will be, will be. They will feel that there is nothing that they can do to change it. Their inner child has been battered and they don't see any hope.

INERTIA

"Even if you are on the right track, you'll get run over if you just sit there."

— WILL ROGERS

Another indication of an injured inner child is a strong sense of inertia. This individual dwells on past hurts and has difficulty getting beyond them in order to move on with their lives. Most of their limited energy is spent on suppressing their feelings. However, the more they dwell on that situation, the harder it is to get past the pain.

EXCESSIVE SELF-CRITICISM

"We are never so disposed to quarrel with others as when we are dissatisfied with ourselves."

— WILLIAM HAZLITT

Another warning sign is self-criticism that is blown out of proportion. Many people are their own biggest fans, as well as their own strictest critics. However, this must be done with moderation. Individuals with a wounded inner child are excessively harsh on themselves. This is often because since their childhood, they have come to believe that they are useless and can't achieve anything. They can become prisoners of self-criticism, constantly blaming themselves for their situation. By contrast, those who want to recover from the damage to their inner child can drive themselves too hard and blame themselves for their failures. This can, at times, turn into complete self-hatred.

FEAR OF FAILURE

"When we give ourselves permission to fail, we, at the same time, give ourselves permission to excel."

— ELOISE RISTAD

If you are scared of failure, it could be your way of showing your injured inner child! There is really nothing wrong with failing. In the words of Henry Ford, *failure is an opportunity to begin again, more intelligently.* Those who fear to fail have often been heavily criticized for failing at an impressionable age, or have been made to believe that winning is everything and there is no room for failure. It becomes impossible for these individuals to accept failure. As a result, they fear failure. Their drive to avoid failure is a manifestation of an injured inner child. Life isn't always perfect. If you realize this, you will understand life better. The fear of failure is not necessarily a motivation for success; it's very likely a sign of a misguided inner child.

These signs are useful indicators, but do not include all of the tools for assessing your inner child. There can be many reasons why we feel insecure or unhappy. They are not all the result of childhood problems. However, if you can identify with three or more of the signs, it is likely that your inner child requires therapy. Having identified and acknowledged your signs, the next challenge is to determine the healing methods to be applied to your injured inner child. You need to start looking at ways to break free from those obstacles and enjoy the positive, fun, and creative side of your inner child.

Chapter Summary

The main focus of this chapter was how to know for sure whether your inner child is hurt or not. We, therefore, covered the following issues:

- Hiding your True Feelings
- Failure to Trust or Believe in Others
- Hiding or Overblowing your Ego
- Insecurity
- Loss of Confidence in Oneself and One's Abilities
- Excessive Worry

- Inertia
- Excessive Self-Criticism
- Fear of Failure

In the next chapter, you will learn: Is Your Hurt Inner Child Affecting Your Relationships?

3

IS YOUR HURT INNER CHILD AFFECTING YOUR RELATIONSHIPS?

Focus: Understanding the signs that the hurt of your inner child is causing setbacks for your relationships.

This inner child is always afraid. It's caught in that time while it was so psychologically wounded that it did not even know what to do. It will follow us from one relationship to another, until we achieve the strength in ourselves to restore and heal this child. Would you like to let go of the old and take control of your future? Give your inner child the ability to heal, instead of bringing it from one relationship to the other.

THE INNER CHILD EXISTS FOR A LIFETIME.

There is always lots of discussion concerning the inner child whenever it comes to individual development, as well as self-healing. However, much of the discussion revolves around a mistaken idea. We can't just acknowledge or move on from our inner child. That is not the case. The inner self is a wounded, but joyful, aspect of our true selves. We must include it in our life not only a single time, but throughout the duration of our trip.

YOUR INNER CHILD WAITS PATIENTLY FOR RESOLUTION AND FOR PEACE.

What is the status of your romantic relationship? Have you had a series of lovers that you have unconditionally loved and respected? Or is your recent relationship characterized by volatility and pain? Our relationships can become toxic and stagnant, if we carry our shattered inner child together with us. Our inner child is patiently waiting for peace and resolution. You will notice a difference in your life when you can achieve this.

HOW INNER CHILDREN WRECK OUR RELATIONSHIPS.

Is the inner child causing you problems in your current relationships? The inner child is often hidden behind it all, when you live in a perpetual state of conflict, destructive behaviors, and toxic manipulation. You must open yourself to all of it and allow it to start opening up with you in all its grief and pain, in order to reach the relationships that bring you peace.

Increased conflict

Is there tension in every relationship you've ever had? When you don't get your way with your lover, do you have temper tantrums? Are you hesitant about finding a middle ground or insisting on having your way with everything? Those are the expectations of a youngster, a child yearning to carve out a place for itself in the world. We can reduce the need for confrontation, by allowing the inner child to break away from loss of control and the fear of being seen.

Toxic patterns

The inner child is constantly attempting to understand (and excuse) the agony it has been subjected to. When it is about relationships, that usually reveals itself in your actions and beliefs. You can be chasing people who remind you of whichever monster lived underneath the bed, if you have a poisonous pattern of chasing unavailable companions. You might even develop an obsessive clinginess, as a result of your dread of being rejected. These destructive tendencies feed off of our wounded inner child, as well as the sorrow we can't let go of.

Artful manipulation

Children do not have much power. In fact, the majority of parents prefer their children to be quiet most of the time. This instills in children the belief that they aren't able to communicate directly with the parent. The inner children learn how to use emotional manipulation as the most successful approach to achieve whatever they want from other people, from dismissive to absolute denial. Nevertheless, this can easily turn into micromanipulation and toxic relationships, whereby we influence and harass our companions instead of being honest with them.

Stifled emotions

What is the present condition of your feelings in your relationships? Do you consider yourself to be stable as well as aware? Or might you share considerably more traumatic experiences from your lifetime with others? The inner children that are broken assist us in creating distorted intimacy. People have a difficult time acknowledging their feelings, let alone processing them on a personal basis. We frequently wipe out our feelings and bury them deep within. Rather than finding satisfaction in the truth, we choose to keep our misconceptions alive.

Avoiding honesty

How do kids in your life deal with disagreements? Do they take a strong stance and embrace it openly? Or do they try to stay away from it? Consider your childhood. Whenever you committed a mistake or damaged anything you were not allowed to, what happened? Did you try to flee and hide? It's the same with your inner child. If we allow this inner side of ourselves to go unchecked for an extended period of time, it starts learning to avoid truthfulness. We also learn how to avoid it. This avoidance manifests itself in our relationships and our unwillingness to stand up when it counts.

Rotating doors

Have you had a revolving door of relationships in your life? Perhaps you are trying to find out what you want, and you are having trouble finding someone who "gets it." This technique may seem reasonable. However, it does not add up if you have never spent some time contemplating (on your own) what matters and what does not. Rather than jumping from one person to the next and destroying several lives, we must first heal and find peace within ourselves.

HEAL YOUR INNER CHILD AND IMPROVE YOUR RELATIONSHIPS

Allow the inner child to recover in order to create more solid, fair, and healthy relationships. It's not a straightforward procedure. It's also neither a one-size-fits-all solution nor a quick fix. You must first embrace who your inner child really is and then provide a secure environment for it to emerge. You must also (to some extent) involve your companions in the healing process and develop more effective strategies to let go of the old and appreciate the present.

1. Accept that your inner child exists

Acceptance is the first step in any healing process. You cannot reach where you are going, unless you first understand where you are. The same is true when it comes to curing the inner child. First, you should acknowledge the existence of the inner child, as well as the fact that you have been hurting for a long time. That is how we encourage ourselves to walk out of the unpleasant delusions we have been suffering from. We open the door and allow our inner child out into the daylight for the very first time, once we embrace it for what it is.

Acknowledge that you have an inner child. Avoid trying to get away from it. Don't ignore it any longer. Stop being embarrassed by it. Each one of us has a wounded or befuddled inner kid. You must first accept it and all of its suffering, if you want it to live in peace.

Would you go past a weeping kid on the streets and ignore it? Empathize and care for your inner child in that same way. It does not make you any less valuable if you acknowledge that something is damaged within you. You get stronger as a result of it. You may acknowledge the experiences, uncover the lessons, then let go when you've realized that your inner child exists. More than this, you might connect with the reality you never envisaged and find some peace on your own.

2. Make it safe for it to come out

Our inner children live in a constant state of anxiety. Emotionally distressing situations shaped them at critical junctures in their lives. These experiences make them unwilling to start opening up. It's difficult to break free from the habits and harmful ideas that have kept them trapped. Nevertheless, they must be exposed. As a result, it is our responsibility to provide a secure environment where people feel comfortable communicating with us, as well as sharing their experiences.

Allow your inner child to emerge and extend its limbs in life as well as in love, by creating a secure space for it to do so. You must console it and embrace it. Aside from that, ensure that you choose partners who allow it to feel healed, wanted and complete again.

Allow the inner child to express its feelings. Pause for a moment and rest with the emotion when it starts to rise. Allow it to share its experiences and all the awful things that have occurred to it with you. Know the time to restrict yourself. When the timer goes off, softly take its hand in yours and guide it away to something exciting and distracting. Keep a journal of your experience. You'll gradually notice a child that is becoming more at ease grasping your hand and returning your love.

3. Let your partner in on the healing

Are you in a long-term or serious relationship? It's difficult to develop a life with someone, while going through serious healing. This is because that recovery is difficult. It has its great moments, but it also has its bad days. As a result, your companion becomes the witness. They see you while you are dealing with the inner child, then they see you when you've overcome your anguish. Whatever you do, you can't refrain from making your companion a participant.

If you are in a committed relationship (and opening up towards your partner with long-term possibilities), it's crucial to let them know you are going through a healing process. That's not to imply we have to expose the whole extent of our suffering. However, we must feel free to let them understand that we're working on something. It's also fine to anticipate compassion from them.

Don't step over any boundaries you are not prepared to step over. A dread of alerting your partner concerning every personal recovery, on the other hand, is a warning indicator. Whenever we tell someone that we care about anything significant to us, we must not feel "strange" or "silly." In fact, if we're connected with the appropriate people, they'll help and support us, even if they don't comprehend (or aren't aware of it). Allow your partner to participate in the recovery process to the extent that you are both comfortable. Allow them to rejoice with you as you progress.

4. Re-parent yourself more effectively

Inner children with damaged hearts are frequently the result of guardians who were themselves broken people. They implanted trauma into the children (either intentionally or unintentionally). We must step in to become the good parents, which these inner children have never seen. This will help to diagnose and treat them. We must teach kids how to maintain emotional stability, as well as better ways to interact with the environment around them.

Be a parent to yourself in the proper manner. Examine the inner child carefully, focusing on the habits and ideologies that are affecting your quality of life the most. How do you instill in it the belief that loving somebody is risk-free? How do you teach children not to lash out at the world and individuals who matter most to them?

Be the caring ear they've never had before. Remove all of their fears and judgments that have been holding them back. Demonstrate what a responsible keeper looks like. Show them somebody that values them as they are, not for what they can accomplish to earn love or respect. It is also important to set limits for them. You should be firm in the most compassionate way possible.

5. Help your inner child let go of the past

As much as anything, your inner child lives in this hazy time in your life. It lashes at you right now, but its emotions and thoughts are rooted in the traumatic experiences of the past.

You must reclaim your inner child from the past and then reintegrate it into your present. It also has every right to be happy about its recovery. Teach it how and where to accept and move on from its experiences, so that it will ultimately be happy.

Assist the inner child in you to let go of the old, along with all of the relationships and people that have wounded you. It was not its responsibility that this happened. It had little impact on the behavior of others around it, and it did nothing to encourage it. It's fine for any of it to stop at this point. It no longer has to be anxious.

Create an environment where your inner kid feels safe enough even to let that go. Believe in yourself to live free of the anguish and resentment that has followed you. Help convince it to come into the present, by promising it a glimpse of what is to come. You can still feel the affection that the inner child yearns for. Out there, in a new family and companions who will embrace you for each and every length that you are, this total and unconditional appreciation exists. Take your inner kid to the center of your happiness and free it from the old, so that you can go forward.

TOOLS TO HEAL YOUR INNER CHILD

Tools and strategies used to heal your inner child can create a personal life filled with peace, passion and happiness. They can also help you develop the skills you need to rediscover that hidden and lost aspect of yourself in relating with others. With these tools, you have a chance to alter your thought patterns to claim a life of abundance.

Healing Strategies

- **Trust** – Your damaged inner child needs to be willing to trust that you will never leave it behind. Your inner child also needs support as you examine abandonment, abuse, and neglect.
- **Validation** – If you are still learning to rationalize the situations in which you were ignored or shamed, you need to accept that those situations damaged your soul. Without full acceptance, it will be hard for you to forgive and move on.
- **Anger** – Anger can help in treating your inner child. By practicing this unintentionally, keep in mind you don't have to scream or be filled with immense rage. You just need to release your anger. Once your anger is released, you will feel better than ever.
- **Loneliness** – To treat your inner child, you have to learn how to interact with other people. Get out of your room and fight loneliness and despair. This will allow you to start to overcome negative feelings and attitudes.

Another great tool for healing your inner child is through archetypical field work. You can practice self-talk. You can also use your imagination. Simply visualize yourself engaging in activities with contentment and strength.

In addition to the actions listed above, you can also heal your child through simple activities. For instance, every morning you could set the intention of trying at least one simple act which will bring joy or fun to your life. Make a list of things that bring you joy. Grab a journal, make a spreadsheet, or make a text document and list them one by one.

To heal the damaged inner child, you need to enjoy your life. You have to remove negative self-talk, feelings, and thoughts. Enjoy your life through doing what you truly want to. For example, you could hang out with your friends, plan an outdoor party, or do something else.

Why Do You Need to Heal Your Inner Child?

There are several reasons why you should heal your inner child. Here are a few benefits of doing so:

- You'll feel more loved and secure.
- Make productive life choices.
- Stop fixating on past life events.
- Feel more blessed and joyful.
- Choose healthier, productive life patterns.
- Learn how to forgive and forget.

Through healing your inner child, your life can turn out great. You can live your life the way you truly want it to be.

For some, treating the inner child can be tough. In particular, if you've faced lots of childhood trauma, abuse, and suffering, it can be more difficult. However, it doesn't mean you have to give up or lose hope. You just need to open your mind and be willing to accept your inner child.

LEARNING TO TRUST

Trust means putting confidence in somebody to be honest and faithful towards you. To trust another requires a genuine perspective about them and an expectation of failure. Trust should also be combined with the willingness to forgive and develop best in an environment of love and acceptance.

Do you understand why not everyone trusts others? According to some, trust should be earned. When broken, it becomes hard for you to trust the person ever again. People don't always believe in others to protect them. They don't want to get hurt and they don't expect much from others around them.

In some instances, although you need to trust somebody, there is something which stops you. You feel as if you can't fully trust that person. Depending on the situation, some people fail to let go of their past heartaches and pains. Whether you believe this or not, restoring lost trust is very possible. How are you able to do this?

Here are a few tips:

- **Know why you should trust again** – Many people delude themselves into thinking they do not have to trust anybody. Nonetheless, humans are ultimately social creatures. Therefore, you can never live completely in solitude and still maintain good health and happiness. Without trust, it's hard to have a close relationship. This is the reason why some people have an empty and desolate life.

- **Accept areas that you exhibit trust** – Let's say, for instance, you had several terrible experiences during childhood. You may think that most people are the same. You prefer not to trust people, so you can avoid the same situations. They might lead to heartache and pain. This perception is erroneous. Not all people are the same. You simply need to give them a second chance to know who they really are. However, some people are indeed toxic or counterproductive to your life, and, in these situations, it would be preferable not to spend much time with them.

- **No one is perfect** – You need to know that no individual will meet all your needs. People keep on trying to find an ideal or perfect mate. This should not be your priority. Whether you trust your friends or relatives, you have to accept the fact that they aren't perfect, just as you are not. They may sometimes let you down or disappoint your expectations. That's just life, but it shouldn't mean those people are wicked or you can never forgive them.

- **Look for individuals who are truthful** – The best indicator of how an individual may treat you, depends on how they treat other people. If they tell you the personal life of others behind their back, it may indicate they are not reliable or could easily betray you.
- **Don't give your trust immediately** – Before you can trust someone, you must first learn about them. You must comprehend their mindsets. You may be frustrated, if you place your confidence in someone you don't really know.
- **Trust yourself first** – Before trusting anyone, always begin with yourself. The fear of trusting others is more likely due to your fear of not being able to manage a betrayal.

Since trusting yourself is so essential, you need to take action to develop your self-trust. Follow through with decisions, be honest, keep commitments, and establish boundaries. These can help in improving self-trust.

LEARNING TO FORGIVE YOURSELF AND OTHERS

Learning to forgive others and forget wrongs is typical advice you might have received from friends, family, or self-help books. It's good advice, but the fact is that many people are unable to forgive those who have hurt them. Some wounds and traumas are too deep. Even though forgiving others is challenging, I am confident you can still do it. You just need to understand how to do it. Here are a few strategies for learning to forgive yourself and others:

1. *Know the difference between forget and forgive* –
   Forget means that you've forgotten the past incidents in your life. However, it doesn't mean that once you forget, you can easily forgive the involved persons. It often takes time to forgive yourself and others, especially when the consequences of the actions are destructive.
2. *Accept reality* – Instead of trying to forget completely, learn how to accept it for what it is. You can do this by asking yourself why and how it happened. To forgive yourself, you must take responsibility for your own actions. To forgive others, you have to hear their side before judging them. Take time to talk to the person who is involved, and learn to move on and accept it for what it is.
3. *Ask forgiveness from others* – If you have made

mistakes, you need to ask forgiveness from others. Make amends to those you have wronged. If possible, talk to them and explain to them what you have done. You could also explain what pushed you to these actions.

4. *Learn how to forgive yourself* – Once you forgive yourself, it is easy for you to accept reality. Other people will prefer to forgive you. By learning how to first forgive yourself, you can more easily accept forgiveness from others and learn to forgive other people, despite any wrongdoing.

5. *Accept your imperfections* – Humans make mistakes. Therefore, you must accept your flaws. Once you make a mistake, you can always ask for forgiveness and correct your future actions. It is also best to stop thinking negatively. Use your mistakes as a way to improve yourself. Yes, you made a mistake. However, you have learned from it and have gained greater self-knowledge.

6. *Seek professional help* – If you can't handle your situation, you may want to seek help from a therapist or counselor. They can help you in continuing the process of self-forgiveness. You can also get books on how to forgive yourself and other people.

With these simple tips, you can learn how to forgive yourself and others. You just need to focus on the things you need to do, and you will get what your inner child truly needs.

Benefits of Forgiving Yourself and Others

Forgiveness is the ability to let go of various flaws in life. It often involves making peace with your friends, relatives and other people. Maybe you will ask, why do you have to forgive yourself and others? Here are a few reasons:

- *Failure to forgive creates a mental block to your success* – If you fail to forgive others, you can create a mental block on your path to success. Therefore, forgiving others will help you to see the real meaning of happiness and contentment.
- *It's crucial for joy and prosperity* – Forgiving yourself and others is a key for ultimate joy and prosperity. It will help you enjoy your life more because you won't have to carry the weight of your or somebody else's past wrongdoing.

As you can see, there are many benefits to forgiving yourself and others. Once you practice a more positive attitude and mindset, you will feel the heartache becoming less intense. It is also easy for you to focus on your goals, rather than spending the time quarrelling.

Chapter Summary

The focus of this chapter was understanding the signs that the hurt of your inner child is causing setbacks for your relationships. We covered the following issues

- The Inner Child Exists for A Lifetime
- Your inner child waits patiently for resolution and peace.
- How Inner Children Wreck Our Relationships
- Increased conflict
- Toxic patterns
- Manipulation
- Stifled emotions
- Avoiding honesty
- Rotating doors
- Healing Your Inner Child and Improve Your Relationships
- Accept that your inner child exists
- Make it safe for it to come out
- Let your partner in on the healing
- Re-parent yourself more effectively
- Help your inner child let go of the past
- Tools To Heal Your Inner Child
- Healing Strategies; Trust, Validation, Anger & Loneliness
- Learning To Trust
- Know why you should trust again
- Accept areas that you exhibit trust

- No one is perfect
- Look for individuals who are truthful
- Don't give your trust immediately
- Trust yourself first
- Learning To Forgive Yourself and Others
- Know the difference between forget and forgive
- Accept reality
- Ask forgiveness from others
- Learn how to forgive yourself
- Accept your imperfections
- Seek professional help
- Benefits of Forgiving Yourself and Others

In the next chapter, you will learn; The Guide to Recovery and Relationship Improvement.

PART II

THE INNER CHILD WORK TOWARDS BETTER RELATIONSHIP WITH SELF AND OTHERS

4

THE GUIDE TO RECOVERY AND RELATIONSHIP IMPROVEMENT

Focus: How to recover the hurt inner child — a step by step process

The inner child can refer in part to your emotional body. According to Carl Jung, this is your "divine child," and according to others, it is your "true self." Human personalities emerge as an outcome of their genetic code, which are their inherited characteristics. They can also be shaped by their environment and experiences. Your childhood is partially dictated by those who raise you, and it can cause scars that may take several years to heal.

In the journey to recover your inner child, it is necessary to identify what archetype of the inner child is yours. This is especially important to help you properly tailor your recovery energy. It is a common mistake to think that what works for a friend, mentor, colleague, sibling, or even one's parents will work for you. This is far from the reality, as far as the inner child is concerned. Every living being possesses a set of distinct experiences and desires that make their inner child unique. It doesn't matter whether you were raised by the same parents, brought up in the same environment at the same time, you are of the same age, attended the same elementary school, or share the same interests as others. Your inner child will definitely be different from theirs. It is against this backdrop that you must understand that you need to address your inner child as an individual entity separate from those of others.

Despite the individuation, however, Carl Jung broadly classifies the human inner child archetypes into six distinct groups. As we launch into the six archetypes in the subsequent paragraphs of this chapter, you will find the group to which your inner child belongs. This will be a bold step in identifying how to help it heal and recover. An understanding of your inner child archetype (with its positive and negative components) will help you to better identify with it as part of your core personality. As a result, you can harness it positively. The inner child always remains with you. It is said that all humans are children at heart. Deep down, most of us have a core of innocence that is always searching for the meaning of life. For you to heal your inner child completely and achieve your desired goals, you need to understand the category that yours falls under.

Here are the variations of the inner child:

TYPES OF INNER CHILD

The Orphan Child Archetype

Some scholars prefer to call this the abandoned child archetype. It is found in individuals who tend to view themselves as independent beings, even at the early stage of their lives when they ought to be under parental care and guidance. It is caused mainly by feelings of loneliness, rejection, abandonment, lack of care, etc. Note that having an orphan child archetype does not necessarily mean that one is an orphan. More often than not, it is the feeling, as the name suggests, that one does not enjoy adequate parental attention and love. Children raised by parents who were too busy with work to create time for their kids often possess this inner child archetype.

The situation could also be literal, in which children were orphaned very early in life. As a result, received little or no parental care during their childhood. Such children may have been conditioned to believe that they're not meant to be loved. Individuals with this archetype are always too reserved, feel isolated and constantly shut others out of their emotions. They also avoid large groups and are almost always alone, if not lonely. On the positive end, however, individuals with the orphan child archetype are quick to develop survival instincts and other life skills, take responsibility for themselves and are generally independent. When the inner child is well-harnessed, they are able to make decisions for themselves and overcome their fears with little or no help from others.

The Wounded Child Archetype

This is also known as the injured child archetype. It is typical of people who have experienced considerable pain and abuse, either physical or emotional, during their formative age. Those who suffer repression and sexual abuse also fall into this category. These abuses might have been inflicted on them by bullies at school, teachers, etc. It is worse when the abuse is repetitive and inflicted upon them by trusted family associates, such as a sibling, relative, or parent. Individuals with this inner child archetype find it hard to forget these traumatic experiences. It also influences how they react to people and situations around them as they become adults. They also become withdrawn and find it difficult to trust others.

In chronic cases, they form stereotypic opinions of others and seldom let go of such opinions throughout their lifetime. They often become used to an abusive relationship and consider themselves no more valuable than objects meant to be used. They nurture hatred and blame their abusers for all of their life failures. In very extreme cases, when they are pushed to the wall, their hatred could grow into unpremeditated deadly attacks on those they see as predators. The positive side to this archetype, however, is that, if they can recover, they redirect their hatred toward care and love for others who are victims of the same situation. They are quick to forgive and show compassion to others who've had the same ugly experiences.

The Nature Child Archetype

If you know a person who really loves nature, it's possible they might have the nature child archetype. Individuals with this archetype are helplessly in love with natural things, such as animals, plants, gardens, streams and the environment at large. They prefer to stay in nature rather than among other people. That is where they find the most comfort, and they enjoy a deep connection with it. They value the time spent in nature and would not exchange it for anything. One might think this is a wonderful way to live, and sometimes it can be. The problem with this archetype is that the love for nature can be excessive, and may affect other aspects of their lives, especially their careers and relationship with others because they always want to be alone in nature. They may pour all their love into animals and have little left for human beings. It is even possible that when this archetype is injured, they could become abusive to people and animals.

The Magical Child Archetype

According to Hugh Magnus MacLeod, everyone is born creative. However, unfortunately, not everyone grows up to become creative or have opportunities to utilize their creativity. This is the inner child archetype that houses the child's freedom to explore one's innate skills and abilities. There is a strong argument that we often don't grow up to become creative or invent ideas. On the contrary, as we grow up that we abandon our creative abilities and ideas. Our potential remains unused. The story is, however, a different one for individuals with the magical child archetype. They were allowed ample freedom to explore during their childhood, and as a result, have seen the magical infiniteness in the world's possibilities.

They believe that everything is possible and that the right way must be found. They are deep thinkers, who believe in the power of the mind to think up ground-breaking ideas that can make the world a better place. They are often inquisitive, carefree and adventurous idealists. As beautiful as this inner child archetype sounds, it has its downside. These individuals could be drawn into their imagination so much, that they lose track of reality. They become lost in a world of fiction, movies, and fairy tales. They could also be dogmatic with their ideas and fail to accept the opinions of others, especially when such opinions differ from theirs or are not idealistic. They could become pessimistic and unnecessarily drawn away from others. They are often recluses, who live in their minds and in the world of ideas.

The Divine Child Archetype

Childhood is most associated with purity. We tend to see it as a time when we're still unspoiled by the blemishes of adulthood. That is exactly what the divine child archetype emphasizes. Adults with this inner child archetype possess childlike innocence, enviable characters, pure hearts, unadulterated love and are often very friendly. This archetype is, therefore, sometimes believed to be most connected to the divine realm. People with this inner child archetype grow to become lovable individuals, and sometimes leaders in the secular and spiritual realms. They love unconditionally and respect people's opinions. They care deeply about those around them and put others first. The negative side attached to this archetype is that it could tilt towards pride and self-elevation, due to its godlike characteristics. These individuals could be overshadowed by negativities, thereby making them intolerant of others around them, and their supposedly ungodly ways of life. They could also find it extremely difficult to check their dislike for those who they consider lesser in rank and dignity than them.

The Eternal Child Archetype

This is the inner child that James Broughton referred to when he said, *"I'm happy to report that my inner child is still ageless."* For individuals with this inner child archetype, life is all rosy and easy- peasy. They are the kind of person who received adequate, if not excessive, parental care during their childhood days. This type of individual is hardly exposed to life's difficulties, and as a result, they come to believe that life is smooth all round. They are perpetually childlike in behavior, in their thinking, and in how they react to situations. They are ageless in mind and spirit and always seek to have fun. More so, they are bent on remaining young and care-free. They do not allow themselves to be burdened by life's responsibilities. Conversely, however, people with the eternal child archetype fail to take full charge of the responsibilities that come with adulthood. They become excessively dependent on others, especially their parents and siblings, and become unreliable. They cannot be trusted with serious tasks at work or in the home. They would rather relinquish their roles to others. Taking on leadership roles at home, work, or in social circles is extremely difficult for them, and most times, they find it difficult to make their own decisions.

By now, you would have discovered which of these arche-types describes you the most. Although you might have found aspects of your personality in three or more or perhaps all of them, you would have found one which relates to you almost perfectly. That is your child archetype. With the knowledge of the positives and negatives associated with your archetype, you can now assess yourself to see if you are in perfect alignment with it. The next stage is to begin to look out for ways to heal your inner child. This inevitably leads you to methods of recovering your inner child.

HEALING THE WOUNDED INNER CHILD

An unfortunate childhood experience is often considered to be one of the main reasons why an adult has trouble dealing with different situations with their own emotions. To such people, the inner child represents a dark and depressing state filled with sad memories. It may seem like keeping the inner child locked away forever is the better option. However, bigger problems will only come out. Many broken relationships and frustrations in life stem from an unresolved past. Therefore, it is important to heal the wounded child. There are several steps that one can take to reclaim the inner child. It requires patience, bravery and love to successfully bring it out from the shadows of the past. In fact, many individuals turn to therapy to help heal their inner child and the burdens of bad childhood memories. However, you can take these steps on your own or with a loved one, so that you too can experience childlike happiness and wonder in your life.

Regain your Inner Child's Trust. If you listen to your inner voice and it always seems to put you down, you need to step forward and change it. This is the first thing that you must do to bring your inner child out from the darkness. Let it know that you are there to protect and to love.

A pessimistic and cold inner voice is a product of all the humiliation, pain, abandonment, and abuse that your past self has experienced. To change your inner voice into becoming your best friend, you must practice the art of positive affirmation. To start, you can browse through many different positive quotes from a book or from the internet and print them out. Place them all around your environment to constantly remind you to stay positive. Some examples of positive affirmation quotes are: "I am strong and fearless," "I am unique and wonderful in my own way," and "I am kind and beautiful." You can also recite these positive affirmations every day and repeat them whenever your inner voice starts to say negative things. By thinking more positively and developing a happier and more content mindset, your inner child will slowly start to trust you again.

Learn to accept the past and look forward to the future. The wounded inner child had a pretty rough past, which is why many individuals prefer to bury it deep within their subconsciousness. However, doing so has drained away much of the liveliness and vigor that come with embracing one's inner child. The better way would be to acknowledge that the past was indeed full of unfortunate experiences unfit for a child, but you are now safe from harm and can learn to be happy again.

Do not feel embarrassed for crying or feeling angry towards the people who treated you badly when you were still a kid. In all likelihood, they did not experience a happy childhood themselves. To make this step easier for you, you can take some time alone somewhere and then speak to your inner child. Assure it that the past was very bad, and those people did not have any right to hurt it. However, it's safe now and the child can enjoy the fun things in life. Coax your inner child to come out and say that you need it because you want this cycle of sadness, loneliness and anger to end.

Let Go of the hurt and sadness. Your inner child will feel safe to come out, once all the pain has gone away. This means that you have learned to accept the darker part of your past, and you are ready to move on to more joyful and memorable experiences in life. One way to really let go of all the burdens from a bad childhood, is to write letters to all of the people who were responsible for hurting you.

Let your heart pour out everything that you have always wanted to say. You can even tell them that they have no right to let an innocent child go through such terrible experiences. You can also write a letter to all the good people who treated you with kindness and love while you were still a child, even the ones who have passed away. Let them know how much you appreciate them and that you will never forget them for as long as you live. You don't need to send the letters to these people because the important thing is for you to let it all out. After writing them, you can throw them into the fire and then let it all go.

Surround yourself with happiness. A childhood often becomes bad because the child is not allowed to express themselves freely. There are many restrictions, followed by hurtful consequences whenever these strict rules are not perfectly adhered to.

Now that you are all grown up, you can create a bright and cheery environment that will compensate for the darkness that your inner child was surrounded with. Paint your room in cheery colors, hang pictures of happier times on the wall and have some of your favorite items to hang. Give yourself some time off to paint, sing happy songs, read stories of adventure and dance in the rain. Allow yourself to enjoy the pleasures that life has to offer.

Embrace your uniqueness. A wounded inner child grew up with the notion that imperfections are bad. They feel insufficient and unaccepted because they think that they are not "good enough." Authoritarian parents are usually the reason behind why the wounded inner child thinks that perfection is normal when, in reality, it is not.

Assure your inner child that their imperfections are what makes them unique. Tell your inner child that it is perfectly alright to fail or to make mistakes because that is how life teaches you a lesson. Whenever you tried your best at doing something, but you somehow fell short compared to society's standards, give yourself a pat on the back for even trying. After that, you stand back up and do it again, but this time even better.

Be Your Inner Child's Best Friend. A wounded child was hurt and bullied by those who were stronger and bigger than them. You can probably recall your childhood experiences of being pushed in the mud or physically hurt by some mean bully. Now that your adult self is the stronger and more powerful version of your little inner child, you can tell your inner child that you have their back. If any bully ever tries to push them again, you will be able to push back.

EXERCISES FOR HEALING THE INNER CHILD

"The older we get, the more we need to heal our inner child."

— JAY SHETTY

Your inner child remains with you for a lifetime. Perhaps it would have been less demanding to nurture, if it came only for a while or on an occasional basis. Fortunately, and unfortunately, this is not the case. Fortunately, because, if visible and significant enough, the inner child contributes positively to your life, influencing your day-to-day development and balances your life in its multiple dimensions (including family, social, career, emotional, and physical). Unfortunately (well, not so unfortunately), if the inner child isn't taking the center stage of your life, you would most definitely suffer deficiencies and failures in most domains of your life. I'm sure you would like to opt for the former. But hold on a sec! There is a clause attached to it!

The inner child is a psycho-synthetic experience that spans all stages of an individual's life. What is the implication of this? Every stage is pivotal in the formation process, and at the same time, every major experience you have at each stage contributes either positively or adversely to your inner child development. This implies that while it is good to have your inner child ageless and active at all times, it is necessary to heal it of the negative influence derived from each stage. This is where your duty lies. Reconnecting with your inner child might be a one-time activity, if you are careful enough to maintain the connection afterwards., However, healing is a continuous process because contaminants will keep coming your way! A thorough healing can only be achieved through careful inner child work.

The inner child work refers to all efforts and activities put in place to identify, analyze and resolve all hurts and negative emotions buried in the subconscious part of an individual by reason of bad events, traumas, situations, and experiences from their childhood. It further involves all the processes by which one rediscovers oneself in terms of your true strengths, skills and traits, all of which were lost to child-hood. The process may be carried out individually or with the assistance of a therapist. However, the ultimate aim is to reconnect an individual to the joy, confidence and freedom which they enjoyed as a child. This will allow them to relate more meaningfully with life and make the best of it for themselves. Inner child work isn't as difficult as it might seem, but it definitely requires commitment.

Based on this need, this chapter includes certain tested and trusted healing exercises that have proven useful and effi-cient for healing the inner child. They will help you to improve your relationship. The recovery process of your inner child is just about to get comprehensive. Come along!

The following exercises have been found to be very effective. After doing all of them, you will discover that by doing these healing exercises, the child inside you will get happier. The child inside you will be healed. That child inside you is growing up safely, just as you want it to. This healing process is not only about physical recovery but also about emotional recovery and spiritual growth.

Identify Your Inner Child

The first step in your inner child healing framework is to identify the specific archetype of your inner child. This is necessary to help you properly tailor your focus and healing process. As mentioned previously, there are six different inner child archetypes, going by Carl Jung's classification: wounded inner child, orphan inner child, divine inner child, nature inner child, magical inner child, and the eternal inner child archetype. Having identified which particular archetype yours belongs to, will put you on the right track to individuate your healing.

Reconnect With Your Inner Child

Re-establishing a working relationship with your inner child is the second stage in the important process of the inner child healing work. Due to the situations and events revolving around us, we tend to lose connection with the inner child from time to time, or even for a long period of time. This makes a reconnection necessary. If you are able to maintain the connection after one or two reconnections, this would make your inner child healing faster and less exacting. The previous chapter discussed the possible ways to establish a reconnection with your childhood. Ensure that you spend ample time with yourself every day, pay more attention to your inner child, focus more on the things that interested you as a child, and, more importantly, avoid toxic people!

Communicate With Your Inner Child

Although this exercise has already been suggested, it is necessary to emphasize its importance to the healing process of your inner child. Everyone values companionship channeled through constant communication. The same applies to your inner child. It wants to feel loved, safe, and supported. If you want a working relationship with it, you must communicate openly and steadily. You wonder how? The following simple techniques will be helpful:

Adopt mantras for yourself. They don't necessarily have to be religious. Any positive statement purposefully directed at your inner child is acceptable. Keep a diary. If you love to write, this is a good way of connecting with your inner child. A simple diary of daily events will help you divulge all your feelings, hurts and emotions. At the same time, it will enable you to identify exactly what your inner child prefers in every situation. Write a letter to your inner child. Letters may not be a daily exercise, but they wield as much influence as keeping a diary. Write down all your childhood desires and interests. It will help to build a bond between you and your inner child.

Take Proper Note of Your Inner Critic

It is common to override the interests of the inner child, while making decisions that pertain to us as adults. You must appreciate that this is a significant way many of us have silenced and suppressed our inner child. Every individual's inner child has a dimension to it that enters into our consciousness and says what it prefers or desires in certain situations. Although many scholars see this dimension as a component of conscience, it is much more delicate than the human conscience. It suggests ideas, dictates preferences, requests attention, and warns against harm. The problem is that, more often than not, we decline all of its requests. To completely recover your inner child, you must pay close attention to what it asks for at each point in time. This involves asking questions and checking on it regularly.

Undergo A Session with A Therapist

This is another effective method of healing the inner child. It involves an expert who sees you not as an adult but as a child willing to explore. Regular sessions with your psychothera-pist, in addition to the other exercises discussed already, will put you on the right road toward recovering your inner child. Although you are in the best position to ascertain your inner child needs, experts will assess your progress and make recommendations, where necessary.

Adopt The 'Play' Technique

The 'play' technique is also frequently used by expert thera-pists. You could adopt it in the comfort of your home. Assemble dolls, toy games, and all the children items you used as a small boy or girl. Although it sounds awkward, this exercise has been found to be one of the most effective because, among other reasons, it is carried out in a relaxed state.

Meditate Regularly

This exercise may be used with mantras. Situate yourself in a comfortable environment free of noises and distractions. Allow your thoughts to flow smoothly on their own and let your mind travel back in time to the sweet moments you enjoyed during your childhood. Practice this regularly. It is a simple method that has been found to effectively reconcile adults with their inner child. The effort to recover one's inner child is a demanding one. It requires willpower, commitment, patience and guidance. Although you can take steps toward achieving this by yourself, it is recommended that you consult an expert psychotherapist for motivation, guidance, and the use of the proper techniques. Your life is in the best shape when you live as a child, free from worries and troubles.

EXERCISE THAT IMPROVES CONNECTING WITH THE INNER CHILD

This healing process is not just about physical recovery. It also involves emotional recovery and spiritual growth. How you improve your relationship with another person, such as your partner, depends on the person and how you both feel about one another. For those who struggle with their relationship, it can seem like an impossible goal. This chapter offers some insight and advice about healing your relationship and relating more easily with one another through your inner child. It is also a unique and original way to relate to one another (especially if you've been in a negative cycle for a very long time). This is not the only way to improve your relationship.

When you heal your inner child, you become more emotionally balanced, and you can regain your power. If you don't like how your relationship is going, it may be time to start healing that childhood pain (or your partner's childhood pain). If you are struggling to find some time to work on your relationship, you can use the following techniques to improve your relationship. You will need some quiet time, where you can be alone with yourself. Sit down on a chair or on the floor with your back straight and your hands in front of you. Begin breathing deeply into the part of your body that feels the most tension. Do this for about five minutes, then breathe out in a relaxed way. Use deep breaths for several minutes, until you feel yourself leaning back just a little bit more than before. Now, pretend that you are about nine years old, and you are in your home. Feel your body slowly sinking into the chair or floor to be like a little kid.

You can now begin to see what's around you (it might be nothing at all). See how it feels to be in this space. Remember that no one else is there but you. Keep breathing deeply for several minutes, until you feel yourself relaxed and loose (it might not happen right away). You can now remember how it felt to be a child, playing with your parents or guardian. You can begin to go back farther and start remembering what it was like to be a baby. Notice how the feelings seem different than they did as a child or teenager. You can even notice how you feel inside of your body, compared to when you were five years old. Illness may have set in early on and changed your life for the worse (just like with an adult). Continue doing this exercise, until you feel yourself in your very earliest memories. You will notice that the more you go back, the harder it may be to stay in that space. It might seem like a burden or something that is eventually going to hurt you. Go back to before four years old and remember how it felt. If you are at the age where you are now trapped in your body, see how it feels to be stuck in that space. Try to feel what it was like to be a baby stuck in a small space.

You will feel yourself getting very upset and angry because you can't move. Try to stay calm inside. You've probably been taught that being angry is not good, but that's fine. Just allow yourself to have strong feelings, without acting out of control. That's very important because you've probably been told to hold your feelings in and also to feel guilty for having them. It might feel like everything is spinning around inside of you and that you've completely lost your mind (or sanity). Try to stay calm while feeling these emotions. At this point, you can start breathing deeply. Make an effort to remember how it felt when someone was actually there for you. See if you can remember what their presence felt like (it could be your mother or father or another family member). Allow yourself to get to know this person and breathe into them, until every part of their body feels like it belongs to you. How does it feel when they actually love you and care about you. Take several minutes to relax inside of this person's love.

See how it feels when others are not there for you. It might be someone in your life who has hurt you deeply in the past, or it may be something that you learned about yourself. Observe these people with your childhood eyes and try to remember what they wanted from you. See if they actually cared about you. This is an exercise that can take up to half an hour (it depends on how far back in time you go). Notice how it feels when others are not there for you (once again). You can see how these people might have treated you badly, or were just indifferent to your needs. You don't have to feel guilt or shame. However, you should understand that these people were being hurt in some way. You can also see how they hurt you. You've had many experiences with these people, which have had a great impact on your life. Try to remember what it all looked like from a child's eye view. You might have been very lonely or stuck in your own pain. This is now in your past and it's time to let go. Try to offer compassion for them, even though they didn't treat you well. Try to recall how it felt inside of you, when they treated you badly. Try to remember if something bad happened to you.

Try to expose these internal feelings because something bad may have happened to you. You may have been abused, or something much worse might have happened. This is one of the reasons why it's good to do this exercise, especially if there are other people who are not aware of your pain. They don't know what you've been through. Do this exercise out loud, if possible. It can be very powerful to say these words out loud to yourself or even others. It can be hard to feel these feelings about someone who has hurt you, but it's important. Once you can say these things about someone who has hurt you, it is possible to forgive them. Although this might be hard to do, it's powerful and can change your life for the better (even if the person is no longer in your life). It is still important to recall how it felt inside of you, when they didn't care about you or didn't love you. Breathe into those feelings and begin to feel them both as an adult and as a child. This might be difficult but try to keep breathing into them. You can see how it felt to be a child and still be rejected by this person, even though they were very close to you.

This exercise is much deeper than just thinking about someone who has hurt you in the past. If you recall being physically abused as a child or an adult, those feelings can cause more harm inside of you. You can see that this wasn't your fault, and you weren't doing anything wrong. It was someone else's problem. The sooner you understand this, the better off you will be. You can use these feelings to change your perspective on things in your life. You will see how powerful they are when you need them most. The more you allow yourself to feel these feelings, the easier it will be to let them go. You won't be stuck feeling them forever. Once you let go of the past, you will begin to see the person with a new perspective.

This is one of the reasons why this powerful exercise is so important to do. These feelings don't go away easily. They might even come back at different points in your life. You may even have experienced hurtful things happening to you as a child, again as an adult. It's okay. Don't be ashamed or feel bad about these feelings. They are all part of your past. You can get finally rid of these feelings, by doing this exercise. This is one of the reasons why you should never forget about your childhood. Whatever you experience later in life, you will always be able to go back to that place in time where you were safe and cared for.

You don't have to feel ashamed of these feelings. They are part of your life, and you learn from them. Recognizing that these mistakes weren't your fault, can help you to take charge of your life. The more you understand yourself, the better off you will be. The more you understand how something has impacted your life, the more powerful it becomes for other things to happen in the future. You can do this exercise to understand how the past has affected the present. Nobody is perfect. Therefore, you must feel these things if they are there. You don't want to believe that other people can't love you or you can't be happy. If you think that way, something bad will happen in your life and everything will go wrong. These feelings don't come from anywhere else, but inside of yourself (except for the negative part of them). This can feel very strange because you aren't used to being in this place. You must get used to and accept these feelings.

Do this exercise at least once a day for a minimum of a week, so you can let go of the old feelings. Once you do this, they will no longer have any power over you. They will still hurt occasionally. However, they will no longer have any hold over your life. Just breathe into them, let them come out, and then let them go. You might even find that you're able to forgive the people who hurt you. This will allow you to move forward with your life.

There is one word of caution, however. If you find that you are accessing very powerful and distressing emotions that may be related to severe childhood abuse, you should do these exercises in the presence of a trained professional therapist. It's possible that the emotions you're releasing will be too difficult to deal with on your own. The therapist will be able to guide and help you with the process.

Chapter Summary

The main focus of this chapter was: How to recover the hurt inner child-- a step by step process

- Types of Inner Child
- The Orphan Child Archetype
- The Wounded Child Archetype
- The Nature Child Archetype
- The Magical Child Archetype
- The Divine Child Archetype
- The Eternal Child Archetype
- Healing the Wounded Inner Child
- Exercises for Healing the Inner Child
- Identify Your Inner Child
- Reconnect With Your Inner Child
- Communicate With Your Inner Child
- Take Proper Note of Your Inner Critic
- Undergo A Session with A Therapist
- Adopt The 'Play' Technique
- Meditate Regularly
- Exercise that Improves Connecting with the Inner Child

In the next chapter, you will learn: Emotional Intelligence (Towards Yourself and Your Inner Child).

5

EMOTIONAL INTELLIGENCE (TOWARDS YOURSELF AND YOUR INNER CHILD)

Focus: How to show yourself understanding through a strong grasp of emotional intelligence.

E motional intelligence is the capacity of a person to recognize their own emotions and the emotions of others around them, tell the difference between various feelings and to properly identify each one. It also involves using the information about emotions to guide their own thoughts and actions, adjust their emotions in order to adapt to the immediate environment and channel emotions towards achieving his or her goals. The term first appeared in the 1960s. However, it wasn't until 1995 that author Daniel Goleman articulated the concept. Emotional intelligence (EI) is sometimes also referred to as emotional quotient (EQ) because researchers like to compare it to general (classic) intelligence (IQ). Numerous studies have shown that people with high emotional intelligence thrive in all areas of life. They tend to enjoy better mental health, have great leadership skills, perform well in their jobs (especially in fields where extensive interpersonal interaction is required), and tend to have stronger relationships.

Emotional intelligence is extremely important. Having high emotional intelligence is akin to understanding what makes people tick. Emotionally intelligent people understand why they feel the way they feel, what their own emotional weaknesses are, and how they can control and use their emotions to get what they want. In other words, emotionally intelligent people are those who have mastered themselves. Empathy is at the core of emotional intelligence. The term empathy refers to a person's ability to connect to their own experiences to understand how others feel. In the real world, our success often depends on our ability to understand others. In addition to mastering themselves, emotionally intelligent individuals have another advantage in life, which is the ability to connect with others on a deeper level. It explains why they are highly likely to succeed in all areas of life.

There are many different methods for measuring emotional intelligence. Some are very technical, while others are fairly straightforward. The Daniel Goleman Method is the most common. It was introduced by the same person who pioneered the concept of emotional intelligence (as we understand it today), and is fairly easy to comprehend. In Goleman's model, an emotionally intelligent person should rate highly for the following qualities:

Self-awareness: which is the ability to understand your own emotions, as well as your strengths and weaknesses.

Self-regulation: this is the ability to control and to channel your "disruptive" emotions and behavioral tendencies and the ability to adapt to a changing social environment.

Social skill: refers to the ability to manage relationships and to influence people.

Empathy: is the ability to be considerate of other people's feelings and to make decisions that accommodate them.

Motivation: which is the ability to be driven to achieve certain goals.

Goleman and many other psychologists have observed that all the qualities of the emotionally intelligent person can be learned. This means that with a concerted effort, you can internalize self-awareness, self-regulation, social skills, empathy, and motivation.

EMOTIONAL INTELLIGENCE FOR SELF-DISCIPLINE

The term emotional intelligence refers to a person's ability to both identify and manage emotions. These emotions could be their own, or they could be the emotions of other people (including loved ones, colleagues, friends, etc.). Psychologists associate emotional intelligence with the three primary skills that are discussed above. These skills include: emotional awareness (which is the ability to accurately identify one's own emotions); emotional control (which is the ability to control one's emotions and to skillfully deploy them in certain situations to one's advantage, particularly where critical thinking and problem-solving are involved); and emotional management (which is the ability to regulate one's emotions in the face of external stimulus, and the ability to positively influence other people's emotional reactions).

Self-discipline is the ability to overcome one's weaknesses, by exercising control over the way one feels in the moment. It's the ability to disregard immediate comfort, in order to pursue what one thinks is right. It is the ability to resist the overwhelming temptation to abandon the right cause of action, no matter how difficult or inconvenient it may be at the moment. Self-discipline is the main trait you need, if you want to overcome the temptation to procrastinate, turn into a slacker, or abandon your goals at first sight of an obstacle. Self-discipline can be manifested in the form of various other positive traits, including perseverance, endurance, planning, restraint, and the ability to see things through to the end.

Self-discipline also encompasses self-control. Humans have an innate desire to have it all. We desire to eat whatever food we want, without regard for the health-related conse-quences. We want to enjoy ourselves, when we know we need to work. We want to daydream, instead of staying focused at work or school. Even in our personal relation-ships, we want to have great moments. However, we hope to avoid the more challenging aspects of relationships. Being self-disciplined means that you need to be able to control your desire for instant gratification (i.e., you need to exercise self-control). We can develop the emotional intelligence necessary to increase our self-discipline. Emotional intelli-gence and self-discipline are intricately linked. Most of the bad decisions we make, are a result of emotional considera-tions instead of logical conclusions. For example, when we choose to eat junk food, we do it because of the way it makes us feel for a few moments. This implies that in order to improve your self-discipline, you have to take steps to improve certain specific aspects of your emotional intel-ligence.

EMOTIONS THAT AFFECT YOU AND YOUR INNER CHILD

Factors that Alleviate Depression

Jealousy

Jealousy is a combination of different emotional reactions to the success of another person. The responses include anger, fear, and anxiety brought about by not having the quality that you are jealous about. There are various reasons for both women and men to become jealous. For example, when a woman believes her rival is more beautiful than her, it is likely to spark some jealousy. However, it is normal for practically everyone to experience some level of resentment. When caring about someone or something important, you may become anxious with the thought of losing the person or that something to somebody else.

Pathological jealousy (also known as morbid jealousy) is different from healthy suspicion, in that it has a high intensity. It is strong and long-lasting. It can be characterized by feelings, such as paranoia and insecurity. An individual can quickly recover from the standard type of jealousy, once they realize it is usually unfounded. However, people who experience pathological jealousy take time to recover. These are people who are highly obsessed with fears. They always look for something to prove what they suspect will finally come to pass. Morbid jealousy is very destructive and unhealthy, especially in relationships. It will prevent you from gaining the success or affection that you are so anxious about. When you suffer from morbid jealousy, it can result in depression, anxiety, self-destructive behaviors, and even suicidal thoughts.

Leading Cause of Jealousy

There are three leading causes of jealousy. One cause is having a poor self-image. You believe that you are not beautiful or handsome and you're ugly. It is likely that you will always experience jealousy towards people that you happen to meet. You will feel that they look much better than you. A second cause of jealousy is a lack of self-confidence. When you doubt your skills or abilities, you will be jealous. If you are confident in your capabilities, you will not be jealous.

Insecurity, especially in relationships, is the third possible cause of jealousy. The insecurity can be due to having a poor self-image or a lack of self-confidence.

Dealing with Jealousy

Jealousy is not necessarily bad. It is normal for human beings to be resentful at times. However, it becomes an issue when you wallow in your jealousy. It can invade and dominate your life. It will result in you always feeling very angry and bitter. Most people feel romantic jealousy. Others feel jealous because of other people's strengths, successes, and healthful lifestyles. The section below has tips to help you deal with jealousy.

The first thing to do is to recognize the type of jealousy you have. When you are aware of it, it will allow you to learn from it. It is possible to use these feeling to inspire you to be better. Rather than getting buried in jealousy, it is essential to try to be positive. You must let everything go, since you do not need those negative emotions in your life. Sit down, breathe in, and imagine the problems flowing. You should then let them go like the wind.

You must also always try to manage your emotions in a healthy manner. It is important to remain calm in every situation, even when things seem negative. You should always try to remind yourself of your positive traits. Everyone has their own strengths and weaknesses. You should be aware when you start feeling jealous, so the feeling does not get out of control.

Depression

Depression can impact your body, moods and thoughts. It causes you to see life differently. It affects how you eat, feel and interact with other people. Depression is a psychological disorder, that is difficult to deal with alone.

If you or someone you know is affected by depression, they should seek medical help. Depression can cause feelings of sadness that can last for an extended period. It causes you to lose interest in important things in your life. When a person is depressed, it does not mean that they have a weakness or are inadequate. It is an illness that requires professional medical help.

Types of Depression

There are three types of depression. The first type is melancholia, which means significant distress. It can last for a long time, if medical help is not sought. People suffering from melancholy experience emotional and physical issues. The second type of depression is bipolar, which is also referred to as manic disorder. It can cause major mood swings. One is likely to feel overexcited at one time, and the next moment, the person feels sad and withdrawn. When it becomes severe, you may experience psychosis and hear or see things that are not there. Dysthymia is the third type of depression. It is an ongoing depression that usually begins when one is a child and can last for many years, if not treated.

There are various types of depression that are categorized by the degree of effect or its duration from the development stage to being completely healed. Fortunately, most depression symptoms are treatable through counseling and antidepressant medications. Bipolar disorder is characterized by either high or low uncontrollable mood swings (Blatt, 64). It is hard to differentiate between bipolar disorder and depression, since most individuals seek treatment when having low moods but not when they have high moods. The premenstrual dysphoric disorder is another type of depression that mostly affects women a few days before and after their menstruation period and is primarily caused by hormonal imbalance. Cyclothymic disorder is another type of depression characterized by slightly higher and lower mood swings. It isn't as intense as bipolar disorder. Persistent depressive disorder is milder, but it is long-term and has a high potential for disrupting one's normal lifestyle.

Causes of Depression

There are several factors that can cause depression. One of the leading causes is genetics. If there is a history of depression in your family, it increases your likelihood of suffering from it.

Another cause of depression is drug and substance abuse. Individuals who abuse drugs have a higher chance of suffering from major depression. Recreational drugs may make you feel better temporarily, but later can cause depression Certain medications, such as anti-retroviral drugs, steroids, and acne drugs can lead to depression. Suffering from a significant illness, such as cancer, can lead to depressive symptoms. Stress and conflict can make you feel tired and physically drained, which can lead to depression. The death of a loved one can also increase the chances of being depressed.

If one has ever experienced sexual, physical, and emotional abuse, it increases the likelihood of being depressed. Serious life events such as divorce, job loss, financial stress, retirement, and loneliness can also lead to depression. Whatever the cause of depression, the most important thing is to seek professional medical help. It can be treated with the right guidance and medication.

How to Treat Depression

Depression is treatable. \When it is diagnosed early, the patient will recover faster. A doctor can assess your condition and discuss the best treatment options. The two most common ways to treat depression are cognitive behavioral therapy and antidepressant medications. Therapy helps to manage stress, improve social relationships and helps the individual to think positively. Antidepressant medications change the electrical and chemical messages that are sent to the brain.

Cognitive therapy can help a person suffering from depression to improve their life. It will allow the individual to feel better, improve their sleep, become more energized, socialize effectively, and think more positively. The process focuses on doing pleasing activities that will make you feel better. If successful, it will make you feel better and reduce or eliminate negative thoughts.

Doctors may prescribe medications to help patients improve their moods, increase their energy levels, and reduce problems associated with anxiety. If the prescribed medication does not improve the patient's symptoms, it may be necessary to try a different medication. The medications will only be effective, if taken as prescribed under a doctor's supervision.

It is always recommended to seek medical advice as soon as you realize you are experiencing the symptoms of depression. It will adversely affect an individual's lifestyle. If left untreated, it may reach a more critical state where it would be extremely difficult to return to a normal mental state. According to a recent WHO study, at least 350 million individuals suffer or are hospitalized from depression globally. In a group of 100 individuals, four suffer from depression. Therefore, approximately 4.6% of the total world population suffers from depression.

These are factors that can result in depression and some methods for treating it. However, what are the exact causes of the condition?

The Exact Causes of Depression

Fear

Fear is a natural feeling that everyone experiences. It is something that you cannot avoid because it is a way of responding to threatening situations. It is easy to confuse fear with worry, anxiety, doubt, panic, and apprehension. The state of being afraid is one of the worst possible feelings. Everyone experiences fear in different ways and everyone is afraid of different things. This makes it challenging to develop an accurate definition of fear.

According to Arther J. Westermayr, fear is related to cowardice and the idea that nobody wants to be subject to scorn. He also defines fear as a collection of sensations and perceptions signaling to you that something is threatening. The most confusing part about fear is that what you might find threatening might not be frightening to someone else. For that reason, to fully understand fear, your definition needs to be centered around physical and internal emotions, such as trembling, increased heartbeat, sweaty palms, shortness of breath, a feeling of despair, and hopelessness.

Most Common Fears

Arachnophobia is the fear of spiders and other arachnids. The main cause of this kind of fear dates back to our ancestors and evolution as a whole. This is because it was believed that the animal posed a threat to the earliest humans, and a fear reaction was adopted to make them wary of this animal. This habit was passed on from generation to generation.

Ophidiophobia is the fear of snakes. This is most commonly due to cultural beliefs and customs, personal experiences, and evolutionary patterns. This phobia can range from mild to severe. It is also known as snake panic disorder. Ophidiophobia isn't curable, but there are ways that you can help control it. As with any panic-type feeling, you should try to remain calm when you encounter a snake. Not getting close to a snake or not looking at the snake is a good, simple solution for someone with this phobia. Being familiar with where snakes live in your area would also be beneficial. People with ophidiophobia will avoid places like forests, jungles, and the savannah, where they believe there are more snakes around.

Acrophobia is the fear of heights. The result of this fear is the possibility of a panic attack, whenever you're in a tall building or any other high place. The origin of this fear is yet to be determined. There is a theory that suggests environmental evolution. We may be conditioned to avoid places where we can injure ourselves due to the danger of a fall.

Aerophobia is the fear of flying. Despite the minimal possibility of a plane crash, the phobia is still exhibited by some people. Some of the characteristics of this phobia may include rapid heartbeat, sweating, trembling, and feeling disoriented. The most common treatment method for this phobia is exposure. The individual is slowly and progressively introduced to flying.

Cynophobia is the fear of dogs. The phobia is mostly caused by personal experiences, such as being bitten by a dog in one's childhood. The fear may continue during adulthood due to the trauma experienced. It may limit a person, such as avoiding walking on a particular street due to the presence of a dog. Daily activities will be affected.

Astraphobia is the fear of thunder and lightning. Some of the common characteristics of this kind of fear are rapid heart rate, shaking, and increased respiration.

Trypanophobia is the fear of injections. This kind of fear usually forces the affected people to avoid injections and doctors at large. Like any other phobia, this kind of phobia is usually characterized by increased heart rate, extreme fear, and at times, one might even faint.

Social phobia, also known as social anxiety phobia, is one that involves the fear of social situations. These kinds of people fear being watched or being humiliated in front of others. Such fear, in most cases, usually develops during puberty and, if not addressed, may continue into adult life. The most common sign is the fear of public speaking.

Agoraphobia is the fear of being alone in a place where escaping seems impossible. Some of the causes are a situation which might trigger a panic attack, such as crowded places. It usually develops during one's thirties and later. It is most common in women.

Mysophobia is the fear of germs and dirt. It can lead to excessive cleaning of places with bacteria and compulsive washing of hands. This kind of person might go to the extent of avoiding contact with other people.

Removing Fear from the Mind

The only way to overcome your fears is to face them. This begins by knowing yourself. It includes your abilities and what you are good at, and most importantly, a backup plan if things do not go as planned. A friend may play the role of a backup plan, as he or she might come in handy. Daily exercise will boost your confidence. Having faith and talking to others will also help. Therapy is another possibility, and one is advised to visit a counselor or therapist.

Stress and Worry

Stress is a natural human response, when faced with challenging situations. Similar to fear, the fight or flight action is triggered by the mind when stress is experienced. Stress might be positive or negative. It is positive when one's objectives are met. Therefore, more adrenaline is produced. For negative stress, depression is always experienced. In severe cases, it can lead to suicide.

What is Worry?

Worry is defined as a feeling of anxiety about a potential problem.

Is Worry the Same as Stress?

There is a difference since stress comes from the pressure of life. By contrast, worrying is thought-based, and it occurs inside the mind of a person.

Emotional Signs of Stress

Depression. It is characterized by a prolonged low mood. Some treatments for depression may include reaching out to professional therapists, going to support groups, or visiting a doctor.

Anxiety. It is primarily categorized by overwhelming dread rather than a feeling of sadness. Some of the solutions to anxiety may include visiting a doctor or reaching out to a mental health professional. Some natural approaches may also be helpful.

Irritability. This is common in people who are stressed. A variety of strategies can help manage anger including anger management classes.

Memory and concentration problems. Individuals often have trouble remembering things, especially when they are stressed. A variety of lifestyle changes and improving one's diet may help.

Mood swings. Some of the solutions may include spending time with friends, enjoying nature, and generally reducing stress.

The Symptoms of Anxiety and Stress

Excessive worrying. This kind of worry is always severe. It makes it very difficult for the person to concentrate on anything useful.

Feeling agitated. This usually happens because your brain believes that you are in danger.

Restlessness. This happens most frequently in children and teens. These are some of the key symptoms that doctors look for.

FACTORS THAT STIMULATE EMOTIONS

What impacts emotions? This is a valid question to ask, if you want to understand and master your emotions. In the context of this chapter, we will be looking at two important things that impact emotions: the brain and social norms/culture. The brain is a master in manipulating emotions. Therefore, even when you think you know the source of your emotions, it could be misleading. We like to think we are in control of our feelings and the triggers behind these feelings. However, the truth is that our brain has a much more important impact than people like to admit. Every single moment, there are many activities going on in your brain. It is the center of all these activities and complex processes. Many processes are involved in how we interpret situations and react to them. Emotions are defined by three important things: cognition, responses, and reaction. The brain determines every one of these activities. This makes us wonder how our brain actually impacts our emotions. What happens in your brain right before you experience an emotion?

Emotions start in the brain. They are a combination of our feelings, the way we process these feelings, and our responses or reactions to those feelings. The primary purpose of emotion, according to Charles Darwin, is to encourage seamless human evolution. In order for us to survive, we have to pass on our genetic information from generation to generation. This is why emotions are important. Recognizing the importance of emotional experiences, the brain takes it upon itself to evaluate stimuli and activate a suitable emotional response to them. The brain reflects and considers the best way to respond to a situation, so that the primary purpose of survival is achieved. It then activates a suitable emotion as a response, to cause the rest of the body to react accordingly. Therefore, when you find yourself reacting to a situation with a response, it is actually your brain triggering the emotion it considers suitable for your survival at that moment in time.

The brain is a vast network of complex processes, which include information processing. One of the brain's primary networks contains neurons that send signals from one part of the brain to the other. These cells or neurons transmit signals through neurotransmitters, which are chemicals we either receive or release in the brain. The neurotransmitters make it possible for one part of the brain to communicate with another part of the brain. Dopamine, norepinephrine, and serotonin are some of the most researched neurotransmitters. Dopamine is the neurotransmitter that affects feelings of pleasure and rewards. It is the chemical that makes you happy, when you do something good. It is released as a reward and gives you a pleasurable and happy feeling. On the other hand, serotonin is the neurotransmitter linked with learning and memory. It is believed to play a critical part in brain cell regeneration. Research has shown that an imbalance in serotonin can lead to an increase in stress, anger, anxiety, and depression. Norepinephrine, on its own, helps modify your moods, by controlling the levels of stress and anxiety.

Long-term or short-term memory is the function of the brain. Our memories dictate and inform our emotions. You get angry when you recall a resentful memory and are happy when you remember a pleasant memory. This is a continual process in the brain. It identifies a past emotion and then places you in a mood based on the emotion. The next time you get angry without knowing why, it may be your brain recalling some painful memory to initiate a negative emotion. How you can override this is to push yourself to think of things that have made you happy in the past. For example, if you are sad, simply thinking of some happy memories can trigger the release of dopamine, which rewards you with feelings of happiness.

Sleep

When do you struggle with sleep the most? It is probably the times you had so much on your mind, and rest seemed to be a far-fetched idea. Anxiety and negative emotions can cause a person to become restless. This has adverse effects on sleep patterns. Quality sleep is one of the prerequisites for a healthy body. When your body is deprived of sleep, it can create a ripple effect that affects you mentally and physically. Sleep loss affects your attention span. You will realize over time that you don't pay enough attention to your work or what others say to you.

Sleep deprivation also prevents the body from strengthening its immune system with the cytokines needed to fight infection. When you don't have enough cytokine in your body, it will take a longer time for you to recover from illnesses. Anxiety, worry, fear, panic attacks, and sadness are some of the negative emotions that affect your ability to sleep peacefully. If you don't find a way to manage these feelings, you will be dealing with more problematic health and physical issues.

Sports

This has been proven to be true over a series of studies. If you want to put your feelings in check, stay away from junk food, eat balanced meals, and get regular exercise. It can be difficult to keep your feelings in check. That is why many people do not make much effort and give up eventually. A person who can effectively manage their emotions and control their feelings will be viewed as having logical reasoning. They will be considered to be an effective conflict handler, with high emotional intelligence, inner peace, and self-confidence.

Food and Drink

When a person is dealing with negative emotions, food is usually the last thing on their mind. It may or may not be intentional for them not to eat. Anxiety is always a precursor for eating disorders. This is true because most people who are diagnosed with eating disorders struggle or may have struggled with stress in the past. Eating disorders are illnesses. The people who experience them develop dysfunctional eating habits. This is usually caused by their anxiety over weight gain and their appearance.

Music

Art is a great way to use non-verbal expression to increase your mental well-being. It is a magical carrier of emotion for humans. We tend to use art to understand the world and make sense of it. However, that is not the only function of art. There are many others. One is dancing; others are relaxation, grief, mourning, and celebration. There are many functions of music, and nearly all of them are our emotions. Music is a great example of an art form that can transform the emotional experience and bring about emotional awareness. If a person is sad all day, and goes to work, comes home, eats dinner, and watches a movie before going to bed, with no other considerations, they are just keeping that sadness inside. You have to do something about it to deal with emotions. Learning to deal with emotions only happens after a person is able to identify their emotions. It's the first step on the path to self-realization.

Relationships

Once you've raised your social awareness skills and learned how to understand what other people are feeling, you are ready to work on maintaining your relationships. This is not an easy job. You will need to use all other areas of emotional intelligence to help you build and maintain them.

Four Things You Need to Know

The first thing that you need to assess and manage is the effect different people have on you. You also need to recognize what they are feeling and the cause for them feeling that way. If you do that, you will be able to make a decision on the best way to communicate with them to achieve the optimal results.

Four different criteria determine the effectiveness of managing relationships:

- Deciding which course of action is the most appropriate for a given situation. This requires you to recognize the current feeling of the other party and the reason behind that feeling. You will probably have several choices based on the research you conducted. Each of them will cause a different reaction. You will also recognize and appropriately manage the effect they have on you.
- Interacting with the other party based on your research.
- The result is what should guide you to choose what to say and how you will communicate your message. That means that your actions come with a particular goal in mind, making managing your relationship an intentional activity.

- Your needs will be what will cause you to want a particular outcome. It might be your personal needs or the needs of your business.

Use of Competency Tips

Certain competencies are mostly related to workplace relationships, but they can also be applied to relations outside of work. The reason you might primarily connect them to your office, is that they have a lot of similarities with leaders.

Goleman defined the competencies including:

Influencing–the ability to persuade other people into doing something that fits your needs or both your needs.
Inspiring–the skill to motivate other people by inspiring them.
Developing–the ability to give useful feedback and help others build their knowledge and skills.
Being a catalyst for change–knowing when change is required and starting the process.
Managing conflicts–the ability to efficiently settle misunderstandings, differences of opinion, or disputes
Creating bonds–building networks and maintaining them.
Collaborating with others–creating effective teams and nurturing them.

You can use each of these competencies to maintain your relationships. However, before you do so, take some time to think about them. The question you should ask yourself is, "Do you perform these competencies right now and are you good at them?" It's always a good idea to write everything down. Think about the various areas of each competency and note what you are doing well and what can be improved. For example, providing feedback for other people is something that you might be doing well right now. You can also write down where you could use some improvement (it might be the same competency, just a different area).

The next step is to think of two actions that will help to develop yourself in that area and write them down. Taking an online course, conducting your own research, reading a book, or trying to mirror the behavior of someone you respect are good choices. Finally, try to actually perform these actions and work on your competencies. You will notice that it will help you to better manage your relationships with others. An example is giving feedback. You are already giving feedback to other people, but you would like to work on it and make it more supportive. You conduct online research and discover some tips. You try to apply them the next time someone asks you for feedback. You will notice that they will appreciate the supportive and constructive feedback, which will improve your relationship with them.

Work Environment

It is clearly not possible to eliminate all difficult situations because of the nature of human interactions and the need to take risks as well as adventures. There are also external factors that are beyond the scope of individual control. Avoiding circumstances that trigger adverse emotions is among the most effective ways to condition the mind to handle setbacks. An example is where an individual feels irritated when a deadline is rapidly approaching. It might help if the person started planning and working earlier, by splitting the work into modules. One can go further and inform colleagues that short deadlines may make the person react adversely. Change the environment where possible to get away from triggers, especially where the triggers are non-human entities. The bottom line is to ensure that the mind is prepared and has little pressure when handling a challenging issue.

It is important to know how to change thoughts. It might appear to be an easy strategy. However, most people struggle to let go of their thoughts. As indicated earlier, thoughts create subsequent emotional reactions. The persistence of current thoughts occurs because the mind is trying to solve pending issues, which is sometimes useful. Through the use of cognitive reappraisal, one can replace adverse thoughts with constructive thoughts. Sticking to negative thoughts could also be linked to low self-esteem.

Positive/Negative Thoughts

The way you interpret different situations is highly influenced by your emotions. When you are excited, you are more likely to view situations with optimism. By contrast, sadness brings about fear and pessimism. Reflect on your emotional filter and take a more realistic stance, by reframing your thoughts. Restructuring your thoughts involves embracing a more positive outlook when pessimism sets in. Not all situations will present themselves with the same level of ease. Sometimes, all you need to do is to step back, look within, and isolate your emotions. That will give you a clear line of thought. While more is required, the bottom line is to stop ruminating on negativity. You can embark on activities that will switch the channel of negativity in your brain, such as taking a walk or carrying out a chore.

INCREASE YOUR EQ

The concept of emotional intelligence or emotional quotient (EQ) is defined as the ability to understand and manage our emotions, and those of those around us, in the most convenient and satisfactory way. Emotional intelligence is based on the ability to communicate effectively with ourselves and with others. These skills are not innate but learned, so we can always improve them. When talking about emotions, it refers to attitudes (that is, beliefs loaded with emotions that predispose us to act in a manner consistent with them), and automatic reactions (not voluntary or conscious) with emotional content.

People with emotional intelligence have the following characteristics:

- They understand their own and others' emotions, desires, and needs and act wisely based on them.
- They manage their feelings and those of others positively and tolerate tensions well.
- They are independent, self-confident, sociable, outgoing, cheerful, and balanced.
- Their emotional life is rich and appropriate.
- When they fall into a bad mood, they know how to get out of it easily without getting caught in their negative emotions.
- They tend to maintain an optimistic view of things and feel comfortable with themselves, their peers, and the kind of life they lead.
- They express their feelings properly, without surrendering to emotional outbursts that they would later have to regret.

DIFFERENCES BETWEEN INTRAPERSONAL AND INTERPERSONAL EMOTIONAL INTELLIGENCE.

Intrapersonal Emotional Intelligence

Intrapersonal emotional intelligence is similar to what we understand by self-esteem, although it focuses on feelings. An important aspect of intrapersonal emotional intelligence is the ability to communicate effectively with ourselves. That means to perceive, organize and remember our experiences, thoughts, and feelings in the ways that are best for us.

This intrapersonal communication is essential to control our emotions, adapt them to the moment or the situation, stop being controlled by them, and be better able to face any setback without altering ourselves negatively. This emotional self-control does not consist in repressing emotions but in keeping them in balance. This is because each emotion has its own function and its adaptive value, provided that it does not become excessive or does not "overflow."

Emotional balance is the desirable alternative to two undesirable opposing attitudes, consisting of 1) repressing or denying our emotions, which would make us inhibited, or 2) letting ourselves be carried away by emotional excesses, such as a self-destructive crush or extreme anger. The search for emotional well-being is a constant effort in the life of any person, although we are often not aware of it. Thus, for example, many of our daily activities, such as watching television, going out with friends, etc., are aimed at reducing our negative emotions and increasing positive ones.

Interpersonal Emotional Intelligence

Interpersonal emotional intelligence is the ability to relate effectively to our emotions and those of others in the field of interpersonal relationships. It includes being able to:

- Adequately express our emotions verbally and nonverbally, taking into account their impact on other people's emotions.
- Help others experience positive emotions and reduce the negative ones (e.g., anger).
- Get interpersonal relationships to help us achieve our goals, realize our desires, and experience as many positive feelings as possible.
- Reduce the negative emotions that interpersonal conflicts can cause us. A key factor in interpersonal emotional intelligence is empathy, which is defined as the ability to understand the feelings of others and put ourselves in the place of the other.

WAYS TO INCREASE THE EMOTIONAL QUOTIENT

Without question, EQ is an attribute that is vital for success in both life and business. Your success is determined by how you handle the problems you are faced with. Without being aware of your emotions and the emotions of others, without regulating the way that you respond with high EQ, without effective social skills and without the determination, motivation, and empathy, you will always find yourself falling short no matter how hard you try.

Conversation Skills

The more we come to understand how humans communicate and how ideas are spread, the more important listening becomes to us. Listening is more than an action. It's a cognitive process of dissecting, digesting, comprehending, and establishing thoughts and events as valid or invalid in our lives. Only by listening can our lives open to newer and more wonderful possibilities. In truth, listening is the core of all communication.

You have learned why listening in communication is important, some steps to start listening better, and how it can improve your relationships and your career. It is now time to start using what you've learned. Hopefully, you already have. You'll be able to see the changes in your relationships because people will treat you differently when you listen more than you speak. They will feel like they're in the presence of someone smart, wise, and sage. They will seek your opinions, thoughts, responses, and viewpoints on matters. Listening is how you grow in wisdom and intelligence. You'll be surprised at its effects on your life.

Final Tips

First of all, take baby steps. Sure, some people you listen to are going to drone on about things that feel meaningless and, in the end, probably are. But remember that everyone shares something for a reason. By listening, you can probably discern the reason for their discontent or interest in what happened.

Secondly, be aware of how much you're speaking or where your mind is. Remember that distractions are the enemy and that sometimes we're our own worst enemies. If you feel like you're dominating the conversation, step back and listen to them. Start asking them questions to encourage them to talk more. Remember that the way to keep you from talking too much is to ask more questions. People love answering them and sharing.

Thirdly, unplug. Seriously, if you ask anyone who has done it and they'll tell you how vastly their life has increased and grown richer in quality. It's not a conspiracy. You'll feel happier, find focusing easier, and realize that you have more time to invest in others if you unplug. Take some baby steps or go full-on cold turkey; whatever you need to do, but cut back in some form. It will make your conversations deeper, richer, and listening will be so much easier.

Human Emotions

Each individual feeling has a different trajectory. There are hundreds of emotions that can make you react and act in a different way. Whereas anger can cause you to lash out at a co-worker or employee, anxiety can cause you to make wrong decisions or panic. That is not something you want to do as a leader. At their core, however, every human reaction stems from eight basic emotions. They are like primary colors building into all those other shades. Everything starts with these feelings.

Anticipation

From the beginning, you have anticipation. It is generally a positively geared emotion that involves looking forward to a specific action or thing. Anticipation is everywhere. You can see it, for instance, when you are in the grocery line to buy yourself chocolate milk. You anticipate owning and drinking that bottle of chocolate milk. At the same time, when you sit in an exam hall, worried about the questions, you tend to look forward to those questions that you will face. This, in turn, means that the emotion can be both positive and negative. However, it is usually positive when the individual is healthy and neutral.

What do we need to know about anticipation as a leader? Well, for one, anticipation, if used properly, can provide a road map of exactly how you need to behave in order to get people to react the way you want them to. Remember, anticipation is not about reaction. It is a precursor to a reaction. It is similar to a crystal ball that shows you several possible actions that lead to specific reactions. All you need to do is pick the reaction you want and act accordingly.

Fear

Fear is a negatively charged emotion that is often considered one of the most powerful emotional forces. Not only does it behave in a more controlling and overwhelming manner, but the emotion is also inherently reactive. It is different from anticipation, in which the emotion is easier to guide and control. What do we need to know about fear as a leader? You need to keep in mind that fear is more than just an emotion. It is similar to a disease that impacts the present and leads you to change how you react in the future. Because this emotion induces panic, it also takes away your ability to think clearly. Once you feel fear, it is hard to get away from it. It does not simply exist; it breeds hatred, envy, or both. Thus, any good leader must know how to be fearless in the face of everything.

Joy

Joy is commonly used to refer to how human beings feel when there are positive things happening around them. Joy itself is a very buoyant emotion. It is usually triggered by success or some sort of happy event, such as the birth of a child. It is the equivalent of a golden star from our limbic system, telling us that we are doing all the right things. Joy can also be a form of encouragement, so that we continue to do things.

Sadness

Joy is often directly contrasted with the emotion of sadness, which is the most common negative feeling. While the former is the result of a sensation of gain, the latter is closely related to the concept of loss, be it material (when you lose your favorite necklace), emotional (a bad breakup or a loss of a loved one), social (loss of fame or social accolades), or even professional (a demotion or a pay cut). The resulting feeling that tends to overpower the mind is a deep sorrow that connects with the need to seek refuge and comfort, as well as protection of the mind and soul from the loss in question. Sadness acts as a base or supplementary emotion for many other common feelings that we deal with, particularly disappointment, pity, and anger.

Anger

Another extremely strong negative emotion is anger. Although it is considered as a secondary feeling, recent studies have shown that the feeling of anger is more dominant than we realize. The emotion tends to arise from a sense of urgency, generally directed at some form of action or injustice that the individual in question believes requires rectification. Anger indicates that the immediate reaction to a situation is the need for some change. It can manifest in many ways, starting from irritation to indignation or even, in extreme cases, rage or fury. A typical misconception regarding anger is that violent outbursts, which are now often known as 'venting,' are good for the individual and a healthy way to rid oneself of rage or anger. Venting is actually like putting a bandage on the emotional condition. It does nothing to solve the problem. The best way to approach anger is with logic. It is important to determine what causes it and why and how this emotion can be dealt with.

Surprise

Surprise is a sense of amazement or wonder that develops or arises from a sudden or unexpected occurrence. It can be both negatively and positively charged. The former can come from the expectation of something that we have projected to take place but still has not, while the latter can result from a positive circumstance that we have not even anticipated. Interestingly, 'surprise' is also one of the most important emotions, regardless of whether it is positive or negative. Surprise stimulates the production of dopamine and acts as a shot of stimulus to the human mind. Surprise also helps us to focus.

Trust

The final primary emotion we deal with is trust. It is your ability to rely on another person or the confidence to depend on someone else or an institution outside of oneself with any sort of positive expectation. We know that trust is a feeling, but is it also really an emotion? It is also an emotional feeder that acts as a base for other emotions, such as interest or rage. Most secondary emotions stem from the existence of trust itself.

Chapter Summary

The main focus of this chapter was to show yourself understanding through a strong grasp of emotional intelligence.

- Emotional Intelligence for Self-Discipline
- Emotions that Affect You and Your Inner Child
- Factors that Alleviate Depression
- Features that Stimulate Emotions
- Increase your EQ
- Intrapersonal Emotional Intelligence
- Interpersonal Emotional Intelligence
- Ways to Increase the Emotional Quotient
- Conversation Skills
- Human Emotions

In the next chapter, you will learn about Emotional Intelligence Towards Others.

6

EMOTIONAL INTELLIGENCE
TOWARDS OTHERS

Focus: How to inculcate the principles of emotional intelligence towards showing understanding to other people.

E motional intelligence isn't just a fad. There is research and power behind it. The top companies in the world base leadership hiring decisions on it. We will examine the pillars that comprise emotional intelligence and describe how you can use them to become a highly successful, influential leader. The assessments referenced in this chapter are also presented at the back of the book. You are encouraged to use them to help you track progress toward your goals. The first step toward becoming an emotionally intelligent leader is understanding the components: self-awareness, self-management, motivation, empathy, and social skill.

From there, you can take ownership over who you are and how you lead.

SELF-AWARENESS

Emotional intelligence begins with self-awareness. It is the art of understanding ourselves and using that knowledge to grow, learn, and improve. To understand how to influence and drive positive change, we need to first know what makes us tick - why we do what we do. At its best, self-awareness gives us a heightened sense of self-confidence, belief in self, and commitment to knowing what our potential is, so we can elevate ourselves to perform at that level. In an essay titled "How Self-Awareness Impacts Your Work," Dr. Daniel Goleman notes, "Emotional self-awareness is a leadership competency that shows up in model after model. These are the leaders attuned to their inner signals, recognizing how their feelings affect them and their job performance. They integrate their guiding values into their work. They can deduce the best course of action. They see the big picture and they're genuine."

Self-awareness is also the most difficult pillar of emotional intelligence to master because it is challenging to truly know ourselves and understand our motivations. We tend to be more comfortable pointing out ways others can change and improve their actions and behaviors. It is much harder to think, plan, and act in ways that will have a transformative impact on our own reinvention. The most significant leadership work requires that we look inward at what we need to improve in ourselves. It is necessary to solicit feedback from people we trust and respect to inform us of how we lead and how it impacts their lives. To get the results that you want and expect of yourself, you need to develop a game plan powered by self-awareness. It should be focused on five elements: your values, passion, purpose, mission, and goals. Your values are the bedrock from which you make decisions and balance priorities. They serve as a constant in the changing world. Your passions guide your life and leaning into them will help you operate and execute in the "red zone," so you can maximize your time spent on growing and optimizing your business.

Your purpose, or your why, as popularized by Simon Sinek, allows you to act intentionally, with the knowledge of what you want. If you align that with your mission (your definition of success), it helps you clarify and do the goal-planning that leads to the desired results and outcomes that make your organization function at a high level. The secret to self-awareness is a willingness to get to know yourself better than you've ever dared. You must be willing to go deep. Ask yourself questions such as: How much time do you spend in reflection each day? How much time do you spend in meditation? How often do you follow your intuition? Our intuition is our spiritual guide that leads us forward. It always seems to know what's right for us. It's the voice we should listen to above the chorus of negative talk from others and the bleak forecasts that come from many modern news outlets. Embedded in our subconscious memories are the experiences and thoughts we've gathered through the years. We tend to have an innate sense of what's right and wrong for us. We're able to recognize in key situations what we should and shouldn't do. The link between self-awareness and intuition is a powerful one.

Self-awareness is also instrumental in helping us combat the vices and distractions that threaten our emotional and mental well-being. Like the proverbial devil on our shoulder, temptations creep into our lives slyly, in the form of enticing offers and alluring pleasures. Only we know how we feel when thoughts and ideas pop into our heads. Should we go out late for that drink? What about investing in our professional development instead of checking up on that website that we know isn't any good for us? Self-awareness positions us to be thoughtful and to reflect on our decisions. It's the opposite of acting impulsively to do things that won't actually help us. This is why self-awareness has become such a valued trait, because the instant gratification of "now, now, now!" surrounds us and can make us very uneasy.

Let's face it: Practicing discipline isn't sexy. Any discipline that we intend to exercise in our lives requires consistency, self-awareness, and a resolute mindset. Discipline is rarely promoted in social media and our culture. It is not because of a lack of need! It is because there's nothing appealing to sell about discipline, even though it powers everyone from gamers to social media stars, solopreneurs, star athletes, and executives. Discipline grounds us and helps us understand what we need to do, when we need to do it, and how that process will help us to achieve what we want.

A lack of self-awareness in leadership can mean losing the organization or at least losing the trust of those in our inner circle. The scary part is that when we're lacking in self-awareness, we can't even perceive or recognize the faults of our actions or inactions. Self-aware leaders also seek feed-back from peers, subordinates, and fellow leaders across industries. This self-awareness leads to mindfulness and deeper analytical thought and reflection that keep us sharp and helps us stay on top of our game. Self-awareness helps us to avoid repeating our mistakes. Once we have gained the value from our mistakes, triumphs, and all our experiences, we're better equipped for anything the future will throw at us.

IMPROVE YOUR SOCIAL EQ WITH VERBAL & NON-VERBAL HINTS

Non-Verbal Clues

We've established in earlier chapters how emotional intelli-gence is the master key to effective friendship and social skills. By tuning into other people's emotions or by empathizing with how they feel, there is a greater chance that you will respond appropriately to create the desired positive result. Thus, our ability to connect with our own and other people's emotions can be a powerful tool in social and leadership situations. Understanding other people, helping overcome stressful situations, motivating your team, negotiating business deals, and building a close-knit social circle becomes easier, when you can use the emotional information you have about them as leverage. It increases situational awareness and our ability to read people. This helps us to make the most positive decision. Here are some verbal and non-verbal factors impacting social-emotional quotient, or our ability to read and deal with people:

Body Language

Research reveals that body language accounts for 50 percent of our communication. You'd wonder why there were words in the first place, if body language accounts for half the communication process. Tuning into a person's body language will help you pick up important signals related to their emotional state and subconscious thoughts or feelings.

Here's a quick cue sheet to reading people's feelings through their body language:

Crossed arms and legs are signals of people creating a subconscious barrier. They are emotionally closed, suspicious, or do not subscribe to your ideas. They aren't open to listening to your views or are uninterested in the topic of conversation. You may have to emotionally open the person up a bit, by changing the topic and then get back to the original topic. The physical act of uncrossing their arms and legs will make them more subconsciously receptive to your ideas.

How can you tell a genuine smile from a fake one? It's all in the eyes. Observe that there's wrinkled skin near the person's eyes forming crow's feet. People often present a happy expression to hide their true feelings. However, if their smile doesn't cause the skin around their eyes and mouth to crinkle, they are most likely not as happy as they are pretending to be. Artificial smiles create wrinkles only around the mouth, while genuine smiles create wrinkles around the sides of the eyes.

When people constantly take their gaze away from you while speaking, they are most likely not being very honest or trying to hide something. Similarly, if a person speaks to you without taking their gaze away from you for long, they may be trying to threaten or intimidate you with their gaze. It is alright to look away periodically. However, shifting your gaze constantly is a red flag.

When you are addressing a group of people, closely observe the ones who are nodding excessively or in a more exaggerated manner. These are the people who are most concerned about your approval. They are anxious about making a positive impression and want to be in your 'good books.'

People who are nervous or anxious tend to fidget with their hands or objects. Other signs of nervousness also include excessive blinking, tapping feet, and constantly running one's hand over the face.

When an entire group walks into the room, how do you analyze who is the leader or decision maker? Quickly observe everyone's posture. The leader will most likely walk with a straight posture, with shoulders pulled out. Subconsciously, they are trying to occupy maximum space to convey authority over their team. Standing straight and pulling back shoulders increases a person's physical frame. It makes them come across as much bigger than they actually are. This is why people in power love to keep this posture to show their influence over a group or place.

Expressions are the windows into a person's emotional state. When a person is amazed or surprised, their eyebrows are raised, and the upper eyelids widen. Similarly, the mouth gapes open. Expressions can often overlap, so watch for micro-expressions that can reveal precise emotions.

For instance, raised eyebrows can also reveal fear. Look for other micro-expression clues to determine the exact emotion. If a person is experiencing fear, the eyebrows will be raised and pulled together with tensed lower eyelids, while the two corners of their lips will appear stretched. Similarly, a person's surprise is expressed by eyebrows pulled up and a lowered jaw. Learn to read the entire face, especially micro-expressions, if you want to learn more about how a person is feeling.

Since micro-expressions occur in fractions of seconds, they are virtually impossible to fake. For instance, notice how when people are being deceptive, their mouths will slightly angle differently. Similarly, their eye movements become more rapid, the nostrils flare a little bit, and they purse their lips together (a subconscious gesture signaling their lips are sealed, or they won't reveal the truth). Since these split expressions are driven by the subconscious, this makes them involuntary, and it is almost impossible to manipulate them.

Enlarged pupils reveal intense emotions, such as excitement, elation, delight, surprise, and interest. When a person is attracted to you or truly delighted to see you, their pupils will involuntarily enlarge.

The direction of a person's feet can also determine what's going on in their mind. Since feet aren't the first thing on anyone's mind, it's harder to manipulate body language related to legs and feet. If a person's feet are pointing away from you, they are subconsciously signaling their need to escape. However, if their feet are pointed towards you, they are interested or in agreement with what you are saying.

Typical signs of frustration and stress are clenched jaws, wrinkled eyebrows, and a tensed neck. The person's words notwithstanding, if you observe any of these signs, he or she may be undergoing a stressful situation that they are trying to conceal. The trick for reading people's emotions accurately is to keep an eye out for a clear mismatch between verbal and non-verbal clues.

Observe a person's walk to tune in to their feelings. People with a heavier gait along with low gravity while moving their legs are most likely hurt, stressed, frustrated, or depressed. People who walk at a slower and more relaxed pace are reflecting upon something. Notice how confident, happy, and goal-oriented people walk swiftly in one direction.

Observing a person's eye movements is a frequently accurate way of gauging how he or she is feeling, since our eye movements are connected to precise brain functions. Our eye movements have an established pattern depending on the brain function or type of information we are trying to access. For example, when a person is caught in an internal conflict or dilemma (to speak the truth or lie), they are more likely to look in the direction of their left collarbone. Darting sideways from one side to another can be a red flag that indicates deception.

Proxemics is a body language subtopic that evaluates how people reveal their feelings and emotions through the physical distance they maintain with other people during the process of face-to-face interaction or communication. It is a very useful non-verbal signal for understanding a person's thought process or state of mind.

Psychologists and body language experts believe that the amount of physical distance we maintain while interacting with a person helps establish the dynamics of our relationship with them or reveals our emotions about them. A person who isn't standing very close to you may not be emotionally open or receptive to you. They may have a tendency to closely guard their emotions or give only a little of themselves to the interaction. Such people may be more emotionally guarded and closed. You may need to make extra effort to get them to drop their guard and feel less intimidated. It may be a defense mechanism against being emotionally hurt or vulnerable. On the other hand, if a person is leaning in your direction, they may subconsciously convey being emotionally open, or they trust you with their feelings. They may also be more interested in what you are speaking about.

Tone

The tone, volume, pitch, and emphasis of a person's voice can help you decode the hints about what they are feeling. For example, if you notice numerous inconsistencies in the tone of their voice as they speak, they are probably very angry, hurt, excited, or nervous. Ever notice how your voice shakes when you speak in a rage or are nervous about something? It can also be a sign the person is lying. Similarly, if a person is speaking louder or softer than their regular volume, something may be amiss. A person's tone is a dead giveaway. Sometimes people say something that sounds like a compliment. However, upon examining their tone closely, you realize the sarcasm and the condescension with which it was uttered.

The tone in which an individual ends their sentence says a lot about what they are trying to convey, even with similar verbal clues. For example, if a person completes their sentence on a raised note, they are doubtful of something or are asking a question. Similarly, if they finish the sentence with a flat tone, they are pronouncing a statement or judgment. Watch out for how people end their sentences to get a clue about their inner feelings. The words people emphasize can help you uncover their true feelings. For example, if a person says, "Have you borrowed the blazer?" while emphasizing 'borrowed,' it indicates their doubt over whether you have borrowed, stolen, or done something else to the blazer. However, if the emphasis is on 'you,' they aren't sure if it is you or someone else who has borrowed the blazer.

For instance, if a person pauses after saying something, it could be because what they just said is extremely important to them, or they truly believe in it. Sometimes, a person pauses to seek validation or feedback from others. The speaker wants to gauge your reaction to what they said, since it is significant for them. When people are in a more emotionally unstable or negative frame of mind (angry, hurt, or upset), their voice tends to be higher pitched or squeaky. They are most likely losing a grip on their emotions or aren't able to regulate their emotions effectively. Notice how, when people are very angry, their voice becomes more screechy and squeakier, as if they are about to cry.

The Speed of a Speech

A person's emotions clearly impact the speed of their speech. It is important to pay attention to how you start talking much faster than your normal rate of speech, or words per minute, when you are angry or upset. A rapid speech can convey lack of organization, uncertainty, or lack of clarity. The person is not very comfortable with speaking and is just trying to finish throwing his or her words. Again, a slower than usual pace translates into low self-confidence, inability to express emotions, inability to come to terms with one's emotions, lack of emotional reassurance, and other similar feelings.

Environmental Clues

A person's immediate environment says a lot about their emotional state. For instance, a messy, unclean, or disorganized space can indicate a lack of clarity of emotions or thoughts. Of course, everything has to be analyzed within a context. Someone may have an unkempt house because he or she is too busy to tidy it up and doesn't have housekeeping help. All of us have certain spaces around us that are inaccessible that we don't really bother cleaning or organizing (the space behind the cupboard or under the bed). These are spaces that we wouldn't usually clean. If such spaces are immaculately clean or organized, it might even indicate anxiety or a disorder (obsessive-compulsive disorder). Well-organized and clean spaces can indicate clarity of emotions or control over one's emotions. The person tends to be more reflective and introverted by nature. Similarly, people who are outwardly focused, or extroverts, are often surrounded by chaos.

This isn't pop psychology. It is based on clear principles of how the environment around us is created through our actions, which themselves are directed by our subconscious thoughts and emotions. For example, using bright, vibrant, and bold prints in your décor or attire can be a sign of confidence, emotional self-assurance, and independence of thought or opinion. Likewise, a home with brighter and more vibrant colors is an indication of being bold, emotionally expressive, and outgoing. These people are not afraid of taking risks and are more than capable of understanding the needs and feelings of other people.

More subtle colors imply inward-directed emotions or an introverted personality. These people may not be too receptive to another person's feelings and emotions. People who hold on to old objects or hoard various objects can be excessively emotional, sensitive, or sentimental. They find it tough to move away from their past emotions or are still ridden by feelings of shame, regret, and guilt related to the past. These are people who latch on to old memories and can't release the emotions that hold them back. When you use these verbal and non-verbal principles to understand people, your social-emotional quotient invariably increases.

WORK PLACE AND EMOTIONAL INTELLIGENCE

There is a segment of society that is particularly engrossed in understanding what emotional intelligence can do for them. That is the business world or the corporate workplace. Hiring managers all over the world are keen to reap the benefits of emotional intelligence. Since the 1990s, there has been extensive research to support the claims that emotional intelligence makes a person a better employee. The baby boomers of the world did not care much for emotional intelligence in the workplace. They simply did their jobs, collected their paychecks, and went home. Today's workplace has changed. Millennials want more from their jobs than a mere paycheck.

Robert Walters, the recruitment company based in the United Kingdom, undertook a survey of millennials that sought to understand various aspects of their jobs and professions. From this survey, the recruitment company was able to determine that millennials are motivated by things that are totally different from what motivated the generations before them. Millennials are not content to settle for a job for the sake of having a job. They want a job that gives them a bigger purpose. Millennials want to feel that they are fulfilled and growing. They want to feel like they are part of a bigger community.

The millennial workforce also wants the freedom to plan their workdays without feeling as though they are under a microscope. They want to be able to be social in the workplace. They want a life outside of work, otherwise referred to as work/life balance. They also want to be rewarded for the things they do through pay increases, promotions, and recognition.

When compared to the older generations, millennials have clearly set a high bar. It is no wonder that hiring managers have sleepless nights trying to determine who is the best fit for their company. Against this dynamic backdrop, it goes without saying that hiring decisions can no longer be only influenced by IQ. While hiring managers still want to hire smart candidates, they are being increasingly swayed by emotional intelligence. In fact, in one survey carried out by Harris Interact for Career Builder, 75 percent of hiring managers said that they would rather hire an employee who is emotionally intelligent over one who has a high IQ. This is not to mean that hiring managers all over the world are united in downplaying book smarts. Rather, it shows that companies have finally come around to the fact that it takes more than knowing about the knowledge contained in books to survive in the current workplace.

Significance of Emotional Intelligence at Workplace

Emotional intelligence in the workplace is not just a fad that people are excited about that will go away after a while. There are true benefits to hiring an emotionally intelligent workforce.

Handle Pressure Better

Just as the workforce of today is different from the workforce of the past, the workplace has also changed. Workplaces tended to be more relaxed. The modern workplace is more cutthroat and pressure filled. With this in mind, hiring managers know that emotionally intelligent employees will be better able to thrive in a pressure-filled environment. That's because they are able to manage their emotions, even when the going gets tough. Imagine an environment where employees are unable to manage their emotions. What is likely to happen when a critical deadline is coming up? There will probably be lots of yelling and scapegoating. That would definitely be a recipe for disaster.

Better Decision Makers

Decision-making is an everyday activity in the business world. You need to make decisions about how to solve client problems, which clients to pitch to, which colleagues to include in particular teams, how to format a report for a client, how to manage your workload efficiently, and a myriad of other decisions. The more emotionally intelligent you are, the more capable you are of making good choices. When you know how to manage your emotions, you are able to make decisions that are not simply emotional. Emotions are good, but they usually aren't very good catalysts in decision-making.

Let's say, for instance, that you are a team leader working to deliver a project for a client. There is one colleague that is very good at performing financial due diligence, a skill that you need for this project. Unfortunately, this colleague does not really like you, for reasons best known to them. They have made this clear, to the extent of being publicly disrespectful. What do you do? A person that is lacking in emotional intelligence might be tempted to engage in a power struggle with this colleague. After all, the colleague should respect the team leader, regardless of their differences.

However, if you are emotionally intelligent, you will devise a way to deal with the colleague. This is because you realize that getting into it with them is only going to ruin the progress of the team. You will figure out a way to play the role of team leader, without giving them an arsenal that they can use against you. Instead of playing their game, you will kill them with kindness. You will be fully invested in being the bigger person, and you will not allow the colleague to drag you down to their level. This is because you are self-aware, self-regulating, motivated from the inside, and well-equipped with the social skills needed to handle a colleague that is behaving like a petulant child.

Handle Conflicts Better

The workplace is a convergence of many personalities. When different personalities meet in one place, there is a high likelihood of clashes. Colleagues will not always get along. You may have potlucks or staff parties every other weekend, yet there will still be differences and conflicts between the employees. In the face of conflict, you need employees that can resolve their differences with as little drama as possible.

More Motivated

Let's say you are a business owner who has worked hard to build your brand and hire a reasonable number of people to work for you. You invested your life savings into starting a company because you believed in your vision and mission. Two years after hiring your employees, you begin to notice that all of them are coming in late, dragging their feet in their delivery to your clients, and sometimes not even showing up for work. Your brand starts to decline. Your clients are no longer satisfied. You feel defeated. Where did you go wrong? – It is possible that you hired employees who were not emotionally intelligent.

Respond Better to Criticism

Imagine having an employee that sulks every time they are criticized about something. How annoying would that be? As an employer, you do not have the energy or time to deal with employees who view feedback as a personal attack. Employees who are emotionally intelligent understand that there will be moments when they need to be corrected. Their self-identity and sense of worth do not depend on what their boss has to say about them. They are secure in themselves and accepting of feedback, both negative and positive. Outside of regular employees, workplaces also benefit from hiring emotionally intelligent managers. These managers are better able to manage teams, communicate the vision of the company, and even resolve conflict. A manager that is low in EQ might cause the failure of the company that they work for. They will try to impose their authority on the rest of the employees using intimidation, threats, and other unwarranted tactics. The same goes for C-suite executives and other management personnel at the workplace.

Chapter Summary

The main focus of this chapter was on how to utilize the principles of emotional intelligence towards showing understanding to other people.

- Self-Awareness
- Improve Your Social EQ with Verbal and Non-Verbal Hints
- Non-Verbal Clues
- Body Language
- Tone
- The Speed of a Speech
- Environmental Clues
- Workplace and Emotional Intelligence
- Significance of Emotional Intelligence at the Workplace
- Handle Pressure Better

- Better Decision Makers
- Handle Conflicts Better
- More Motivated
- Respond Better to Criticism

In the next chapter, you will learn; Self Compassion, Not Self-Pity.

PART III

TIPS FOR STAYING ON TOP OF YOUR GAME

7

SELF-COMPASSION, NOT
SELF-PITY

Focus: Understanding the difference between self-compassion and self-pity to avoid falling into the trap.

The essence of trauma is separate from the self. In order to make the inner child part of you and your spiritual essence, you have to look after yourself. If you want to use the analogy of being a parent, you have to become the parent. You have to start to deal with all of the things that are going on in your life and be responsible and accountable. Stop comparing, criticizing, and being judgmental about yourself. Stop looking around and worrying what other people think and speak. You have to think about that first. Are you a person who can parent a child and be compassionate? Are you being self-responsible and being accountable for what you think and what you say? The number one thing is your self-talk and your self-image. Please do not believe that because you are experiencing negative self-talk and no one is listening, the things you say to yourself do not really matter. Your self-talk is your mantra and your affirmations. Therefore, be careful what you are affirming inside, not outside. When you engage in self-talk, it is a conversation with the universe, which is listening to you. It has a dramatic effect on you. You cannot do this work if you do not get this first stage right by being truthful and honest with yourself, treating yourself with integrity.

The adult part of you, your mind, is making sure that you are balanced, truthful, living, and thinking authentically, not lying to yourself and not criticizing yourself. So, what you say is almost like going to parenting night school to make sure that you are 100% balanced in your daily adult life. It is almost like prep work. It is putting your emotional house in order, so you can be a good parent as you embark upon this parenting care journey by contacting and communicating with your inner child. The number one thing is self-talk. This is where the cracks appear. This is the first bit that goes wrong with self-talk. It should always be truthful with the highest integrity. What you say to yourself, you should be able to say out loud now. Think about your self-talk. Could you speak that self-talk out loud so other people could hear it? And a lot of people almost create this duality again. What they say to themselves, they would not say aloud. If you do not get that first bit right and you want to be a parent, you have to do the work to become a parent. Respect yourself and have high integrity about what you say and what you do. Have a clear intention, but above all, you know this is about being self-responsible and accountable for yourself and what you think.

Take full responsibility. That word cannot be emphasized enough. Do not look around to blame other people or worry about what they are thinking and saying. Take responsibility for yourself. That is the first step. Please try that. It's going to take you a while. No one expects you to do it quickly, but do it with earnest intentions, and you will realize just how your self-talk is. Many of us have terrible self-talk. It is important to evolve and grow.

It is necessary to be more authentic, truthful, and balanced. This is really about learning to connect more and amplify the voice of our higher self, our spiritual self, our true essence, or whatever you wish to call it. Many adults have let the voice of the inner child dominate, and they have been guided by the inner child. They have ignored the authenticity, highest soul, and divine energy, of who they are. Step One is an exercise in reconnecting to the spiritual essence of you, the authentic part. Many spiritual teachings talk about this part. It is essential to reconnect to that spiritual energy, which is the mother and feminine energy. This is the best place to educate, guide, nurture and support the child's energy, which is the human energy, and the human-centered mind energy. If this is done, the two of them will work together.

That spiritual energy is the loving mother that looks after the child with compassion. The French philosopher, Pierre Teilhard De Chardin, said, "We are not human beings having a spiritual experience. We are spiritual beings having a human experience." It is necessary to choose if we believe we are humans having spiritual experiences or if we are spiritual beings having human experiences. It is believed that all spiritual beings, the spiritual essence of ourselves, or the higher self, is the mother energy. To do this reparenting work, you must get fit. You have to clear out your deck and you have to brace yourself because the next step is about when you start addressing the child.

The first thing the inner child will do is to test you, just like any child. For a long time, you have not been listening to the child; you have been ignoring what the child has been saying. Tell the child, "Right now, things are going to change." Do you think the child is going to say, "Oh okay, that's fine"? The child does not do that, so the first step is to get your house in order. The second step is reparenting. You can now start to work with a child. Those of you who are reading this and have children, let's just say you always let your child stay up late until 11 o'clock at night. You have never said anything to them before. They could go to bed whenever they wanted and they could play computer games in their bedroom. All of sudden, you think it would be a good idea, if they went to bed at 8 o'clock. Do you think when you say the child's bedtime is 8 o'clock that they would say, "Oh okay, Mom and Dad. That's a great idea, I'll go to bed"? No, the child will push back. Therefore, the second step is re-educating your child. That is the moment for some compassionate self-discipline. This does not mean that you should start beating your inner child or to be harsh with your inner child. You know that does not work. You simply have to think about creating some boundaries or some foundations and doing some training.

You have to build trust and mutual respect. If you cannot have mutual respect, you have not done stage one. When you are a respectful character, you say what you mean, and you speak with honesty and integrity. You speak truthfully, so if you say something like that to a child, if you said to your physical child, "Bedtime is 8 o'clock," then 8 o'clock comes and the child has a temper tantrum, you say, "All right, you can stay up for half an hour," then you have lost that integrity. It is the same idea with reparenting yourself. You have to work stages one and two with your inner child. Compassionate self-discipline is working with your child to bring the child and the adult back together. Step two is placing some ground rules for the child. Before, you were letting the child pull you all around the place, so your emotional energy was swinging in all directions. You are now trying to bring things back into balance, by putting down some ground rules. This is going to be healthy for you as both parent and child in a holistic sense.

The important thing is that you are prepared for the resistance. The whole point of compassionate self-discipline is that the child will resist it. They will offer complete resistance the first time you try it. The second time you try, the child will resist and will find a way out. You will want to avoid it. The child wants to give up. It might also give you all the reasons why they should not do what you are suggesting, by telling you why it is too difficult, impossible, not going to be helpful, and why it would be easier to do it another way. You will also hear the lies: "You are not good enough," "You cannot cope," "You are not lovable," "You are vulnerable," and more. However, you have heard this before. This is how the inner child controls you, which is why you must deal with it first. You have to be strong and stand up to the child. You are not beating up the child, but you are showing him/her that you are now in control. It is doing groundwork, by strengthening and reconnecting your spiritual essence, reconnecting to your authenticity, and reconnecting to your intention. This work is worth it, despite the resistance you know you are going to get initially. This is like planting the roots which give you stability, so when you get the push back from the inner child, you can stand firmly rooted and be compassionately firm with the child.

Compassionate self-discipline means not giving in. You have two alternatives: you either do this work, or you carry on down the road of going around and around. It will not heal itself. No one else can do it for you. Therefore, if you are constantly looking for external validation, external approval, external praise and love, then this is the problem. You are not taking self-responsibility. You stay on the carousel of despair, going around and around, "Poor me! I am not good enough. I cannot cope. I am unlovable." The child will want you on that carousel because the child likes the familiarity. The child is used to it. The child does not like the unknown. When you start to give something like self-discipline, which was never given before, the child is going to fight back. This is where you must do stage one. Make sure you are ready for this and that you are firm because you will not get it right. You must be self-compassionate with yourself and accept that you are not perfect. You will inevitably not get everything right. You will also not get the inner child to work with you the way you would like it to. All of these things are the fear in the first few stages. You must try again the next day because you know you are rooted and grounded in the knowledge that this process is worth it.

This second stage can affect your emotions the most. That's why you are engaging with your inner child and bringing them into one. This is because your child has a direct connection to your emotions. That's when you will start using words like fearful, scared, and overwhelmed. That is why completing stage one is the most important. Getting yourself fit to do this first stage, is like getting fit and training to run a marathon. This is the marathon now. This is where you and the child have to work hard for a while because the child will not give up easily. We've spoken about this many times. One of the qualities of the child is determination. They are…stubborn. The child is *very* stubborn and will not give in. The child does not like the unknown and wants to push you down. The child wants you to give up. In the past, you have always given up. The child thinks if they keep on pushing, you will give up, and you will let them have their way. That's why stage one is very important, and requires your total focus.

SELF-PITY OR BEING COMPASSIONATE

Being mindful of how we treat ourselves will be the same measuring device that we use on others. It gets tiring 'ruling with an iron fist.' We cannot move forward without acknowledging the past hurts and dealing with them. We then get to create new dynamics through causes, conditions, and skillful compassion for ourselves and others. When looking at the suffering of others, you can instantly feel their pain, which breaks your heart. It is also possible at the same time to step into your role as an observer and see how things should be. The art of compassion is balancing both these positions without denying either. If you deny and ignore the obvious suffering of earthly existence, it is easy to avoid any responsibility for making changes. People can shield their emotions, by closing their hearts and choose to live in a state of nihilism. However, if you try too hard to save the world, you feed the powers which fuel the suffering in the first place!

Too much or too little is equally as damaging, as you consider the whole that you are a part of.

Having an open heart requires you to strike a balance between feeling the pain of another's suffering and not losing oneself in despair or denial. This creates a perfect recipe for compassion. This will allow you to uplift other people and help ease suffering without having to become a hero. The savior complex results when pity is mistaken for compassion. Pitying another person involves a degree of separation from them. When we pity someone, we see ourselves as slightly better than or more advanced than them. This makes it difficult for us to understand the position that they are in. To be compassionate, it is necessary to feel the suffering as our own because we recognize:

1. We ARE a part of every problem and solution and,
2. We see helping another as a way to help ourselves be better people.

It follows that we do not act compassionately out of any external moral principle or cultural value system. We act compassionately because, once we are whole inside (peaceful), then we feel for others and want to help them without losing the balance discussed above.

Mindfulness and Compassion

Being compassionate is not always easy. Many people don't succeed being compassionate all the time. However, we can help ourselves by building a solid foundation of mindfulness. Research shows mindfulness meditation shrinks the amygdala, which is the part of the brain that drives the fight-or-flight response. This is the part of our brain which drives our fear responses based on past experiences. When the amygdala shrinks, we spend less time worrying about our own lives and become more aware of other people's needs. Happier people who are less anxious and stressed are more likely to engage in charitable activities.

We can observe this in our lives all the time. When we're happy and at peace, we are more likely to smile at strangers, hold the door open for someone, or pick up a piece of trash on the road. When we're deeply caught up worrying about our own lives, we may forget to smile and might not even notice the other person or piece of litter. We don't become worse human beings. However, in the absence of presence, we do not have the capacity to show compassion or empathy towards needs or feelings. This applies to both ourselves or others (seen or unseen). Mindfulness has also been found to reduce activity in the brain's default mode network. This is the part of the brain responsible for the construction of the self. It also includes all metacognitive processes, such as self-reflection, the experience of having a self which persists through time, and the ability to mentally perceive the past and the future. This affects the part of the brain which maintains the boundaries between the self and the world and keeps us from having compassion and unconditional love.

Mindfulness dissolves these boundaries and helps the individual to experience a feeling of unity with the external world, without losing the whole self. This allows compassion to flow almost instantly. The less old ego we show, the more we seek to serve. It then becomes natural to help other people.

Mindfulness Beyond Meditation

Every spiritual tradition across time and space has repeated the same piece of wisdom in different ways, "Be present in the moment." This is because being present is the only way to alleviate suffering, encounter peace, experience divine union, reside in all-encompassing love, and create positive merit instead of negative karma.

Our lives are made up of what we do each day.

— KOLEE

You may have remembered this phrase from other parts of this book. The present moment creates our past and our future! Take a moment to contemplate this idea. The present is where all things are created. We make beauty and fresh- ness as we stay in the moment and repeat the correct actions. After parenting ourselves appropriately, we can stay in the beneficial flow of what we've successfully created and enjoy life, maybe for the first time ever!

According to Buddhist thought, all suffering exists when the mind dwells on the future or the past. Dwelling on the past or the future leads us into varying degrees of delusion. Isn't it more empowering to deal with what is right now and hold the power to change both the past and future? The new reborn ego enjoys this power, while the old balks at it. See what thoughts or feelings arise even now as we're covering this topic! See if the mind aims to protect us by defaulting to transfer responsibility, OR are we feeling excited and ready to do new things?

The old self believes we can never be happy, until we receive certain things in the future. The new self takes the proverbial bull by the horns and rides the beast. It creates that which it seeks NOW! We learn to do different things which match our current view, adjusting what seems to work and what does not, in order to have all we desire today. Being fully present in the moment is the only way to come out of the conditioned thought streams and dwell in our body and our heart. Being present is the only way to experience sustainable peace, despite what lies in the past or the future. While meditation is the most effective path to becoming present, it goes beyond that. Most meditation teachers will advise you to maintain your practice outside of the specific times when you sit and formally meditate. Once we can develop our mindfulness throughout the day, we can begin to find presence in every other aspect of our lives.

Here are some valuable tips for cultivating presence beyond formal meditation sessions each day:

1. **Pay attention to the senses**

Our senses take in information based on stimuli that exist exclusively in the present moment. Our eyes can't see what they saw yesterday and won't see now what they will tomorrow. By paying attention to the data coming in through the senses, we are forced to become present. When performing mundane activities like brushing your teeth or driving your car, you should pay attention to how your body feels at that moment. What sounds do you hear? What are your eyes looking at? What are the smells, etc.? Similarly, when you start to disassociate from your earth body, you should use the senses to bring you back to your present self - like feeling the warmth from a cup of tea, noticing the softness of a blanket around me, splashing cold water on your face, etc.

2. **Focus on the breath**

The quickest way to enter the present is to focus on your breathing and stay there. Checking on the breath at different points in the day can not only help us become present but release any stress or tension we might be holding. You can take mindfulness breaks throughout the day. It is possible to even set alarms for random times, while starting this new habit. It is recommended that you take a step back from what you are doing and thinking and take five conscious belly breaths. If your mind is all over the place and your breath is shallow, take five breaths. It will calm down your body and you will become more centered and present. You will be able to return to your task feeling more refreshed and focused.

3. **Starting and ending activities mindfully**

Before starting any new activity, take a few moments to focus on your breath, find silence, and set an intention for how to approach the activity. When you start each action in a state of calm focus, it will change your entire day. It is a process of cleaning your mess before starting a new thing. You are clearing your mental and emotional energy to plant seeds of purity, instead of sterile or tampered ones.

4. **Give gratitude**

Gratitude is the most effective way to release thoughts that revolve around attachment and aversion. It brings us directly into the present moment and helps us focus on what we appreciate about it. Keep a gratitude journal, where you should note three things you're grateful for every day. Over time, you become more attuned to what you appreciate in your life. You can take a moment several times a day to thank someone around you. When we stay grateful for our present life, we become immune to regret of the past or fear of the future.

Take gratitude breaks throughout the day. You start to notice all the little things you're not happy with (such as a messy house while your children play video games and you are hard at work). Remember how cute they are, how much joy they bring to your life, how blessed you are to work from home while having your children with you, how they won't always be this age, and, one day will have left home. This is a super-powerful pro tip to help us stay present and happy.

5. **Spend time with loved ones mindfully**

Ram Dass says,

"It's interesting how when you give another human being, your family, or your business, the fullness of your Being at any moment, a little is enough; while when you give them half of it because you are time bound with your mind, there's never enough. You begin to hear the secret, that being fully in the present moment is the greatest gift you can give to each situation."

— RAM DASS

When you do this, you notice that your relationships change. You are less irritable, more loving, and able to help your loved ones. However short, you realize the time you spent together worked to bring you closer in love because you are not wandering off elsewhere in your mind. Your family should have a rule that no devices are allowed when eating together or when doing things together. We eat together, play together, and talk together! It's a miracle to have us all together doing the same thing at one time, and when we aim to all be present in the connected space, we interact and share thoughts and stories from our day - enjoying our present selves. Set up a time to work, a time to relax, and a time to truly be present with those around us. There should be no room for guilt, distraction, or excuses.

6. Take mindful breaks

For those who study or use their brains most of the day, this is essential to schedule. When we engage in intellectual work, it becomes vital during our breaks to give our brains a proper rest. It could involve taking a walk in nature, listening to music, meditating, sitting and staring, etc. If we spend our breaks on social media or distracted, our brains do not get a break. We return to our tasks more drained than before. These breaks are CRUCIAL to our liberation, moving from being mindless to being present.

7. Dedicated fun time or creative time

As stated before, when we create our own schedules, we alleviate the rebellious or resistant 'inner child.' We lose all the stories and attachments of the old self and easily slide into the new patterns. We are taking this time in our day when nothing is allowed to exist but leisure, fun, laughter, and creativity. It is a great practice that propels all our other efforts to unfold naturally. When you begin to take downtime seriously, you notice your entire sense of well-being improve. You use this time to lose yourself in the moment through art, music, or fun time with family and friends. You actually take a whole 24-hour period each week to do whatever you want, whenever you want to do it. You enjoy staying on the schedule you created for yourself. You also enjoy breaking from the schedule and allowing whatever comes up to be.

Nothing exists apart from the present moment. If you can't experience joy and peace right now, then chances are, you never will.

SELF-PITY

Self-pity is when you focus all your attention and energy on what is wrong with yourself. This can lead to blaming yourself for everything. You wallow and feel sorry for yourself. It's an attitude that we all instinctively understand will make us miserable. Self-compassion is when you focus on your own limits and struggles but also see the good in yourself. It includes finding meaning in setbacks to maintain hope in the future. It also involves being kind and understanding toward yourself, which leads to a happier perspective. Research shows that self-compassion is associated with positive outcomes, such as happiness and motivation. When you have self-compassion, you don't have to do anything or become anything to be worthy of love or belonging. You simply are who you are right now, right here. Self-pity is a downward spiral of negativity and despair. It will cause you to doubt yourself and your capabilities, and leave you feeling hopeless, sad, and angry.

Self-compassion is something that can be developed. However, you need to have first developed the capacity for it before focusing on it. You first have to be able to look at yourself, make a judgment, and then see your shortcomings without being upset by them. If you are able to accept yourself as you are right now, it will allow you to develop self-compassion. It will ultimately help you to have a more positive outlook on life. It is a positive emotion that helps you better deal with stress and adversity, and can improve your physical and mental health. Self-compassion involves taking a balanced approach to our thoughts and feelings in difficult situations. It is a non-judgmental form of self-love that allows us to acknowledge when we have hurt ourselves, when we have been rejected or when we have failed or made mistakes. We all need this human emotion that helps us deal with the difficulties in life in a healthy way.

It has been found that self-compassion is associated with a number of positive outcomes, including lower levels of depression and anxiety, as well as increased life satisfaction and gratitude. Research has also found that it can reduce feelings of shame and guilt, lower our expectations for ourselves, and improve empathy for others. The research also shows that those who have higher levels of self-compassion tend to be more resilient in the face of stress, take more action to improve their well-being, and are more creative and focused in achieving their goals. Over time, having a more compassionate view of oneself can have a positive impact on the quality of our lives.

It's quite natural for us to get angry or upset, when things don't work out how we want them to. It can be hard to cope with disappointments in our lives, and these feelings can often cause negative emotions, which, in turn, lead to self-judgment and depression. This can be caused by our thoughts and attitudes because, when we feel angry or upset, the way we perceive things tends to change. If we tend to be self-critical, negative thoughts about ourselves will often prevail. This can lead us to feel shameful, guilty, anxious, or depressed. The way we feel about ourselves can also change when we feel like a failure or don't like our body image. We may compare ourselves to others, which usually leaves us feeling down.

When we feel down about ourselves, we tend to invent untrue stories about why we feel that way. We could tell ourselves that we are no good, we are stupid and ugly, and we don't deserve anything better. According to Dr. Kristin Neff, self-compassion is an alternative form of self-love that means accepting and caring for yourself rather than being harshly self-critical. It involves seeing your failures and weaknesses as part of the human condition. We all have them and accepting that helps us to take better action in the future. When we care about ourselves but don't feel bad about ourselves, we are more likely to be at our very best.

It's easy to focus on negative things when things don't go our way or when we make mistakes. Self-pity is one way of feeling this way, rather than taking an objective view of the situation and accepting it for what it is. We do this because we want to see things as they really are and be realistic and honest with ourselves and others. However, when we focus on the bad over the good, it limits our ability to feel happiness. Those who are self-compassionate come across as highly compassionate towards others, but they aren't. They still notice their shortcomings, weaknesses, and mistakes like anyone else would. However, they don't beat themselves up over them. They allow themselves to feel down about it briefly, if need be, but then they move on.

Self-pity doesn't make us happy in the long run. This is because once we start this ingrained habit, if we're still unable to change, we will always feel the need to be in a bad mood. It can lead us to become depressed and introverted because it isn't a positive state of mind. Focusing on self-pity will then put a damper on our lives and take away from our feelings of happiness and joy. Those who are self-compassionate don't have to suffer from feelings of self-pity because they are able to deal with their emotions in a more positive way.

Compassion is being kind and understanding toward ourselves when we face setbacks. It allows us to be content with how things are right now, without feeling ashamed or guilty about it. Self-compassion also allows us to take good care of ourselves by eating healthy foods and getting enough sleep without beating ourselves up over it. Self-compassion is about developing a more balanced view of ourselves. Rather than being harsh on ourselves when we make mistakes, we see them as part of our human condition.

Self-pity and self-criticism can be a part of our daily lives. However, it is something we should be aware of and work to remove from our thoughts and feelings. Focusing on our mistakes and failures can lead to depression and self-loathing. It's only when we realize that everything in life goes wrong occasionally that we can stay true to ourselves and develop a more positive outlook on the situation. We all make mistakes, and when we accept this truth, we can feel happy and content with life. We can then turn our focus on to positivity and not be a victim of negativity.

Self-pity is also a sign of low self-esteem, which is the opposite of self-love that helps us to improve the way we feel about ourselves. Recognizing this feeling is important because it is an indication that our thoughts are not helping us. It won't allow us to become more confident, better, or happier people, if we continue with it. Self-compassion is something that can help us deal with our mistakes and failures in a more effective way. This makes it easier to accept things as they are, instead of concentrating on our shortcomings. It allows us to improve the way we feel about ourselves and focus on positive measures that will lead us to success. Here are some ways to help you move away from

174 | DON BARLOW

self-pity and develop a more compassionate attitude towards yourself.

1. Look at things objectively without any preconceived ideas. Try to remember the last day, hour, week, or month wasn't so bad because you have your strengths, talents, and weaknesses just like everyone else. There are always things that are beyond our control. Looking at the bright side of life will give us a more balanced view of ourselves and others around us.

2. Talk to someone about how you feel. It could be a friend, family member, or psychologist. Asking for help doesn't mean you're weak. It means you're strong because it shows that you are not willing to suffer in silence anymore. You want to solve your problems, so that life becomes happier and more enjoyable.

3. Go outdoors and enjoy nature. The outdoors is there for us to feel better about ourselves, clear our minds, and simply be present in the world. When you are outdoors, your mind is less likely to be occupied by things that are worrying you, so less time will be spent dwelling on them.

4. Make a list of the things you're good at and that make you successful in life. Don't focus on your weaknesses. This can only have a negative effect on your self-esteem and self-confidence. Listing your

strengths will help you to build upon them and work on your weaknesses more effectively.

5. Write the following affirmation in the form of a prayer for each day of the week: "I have enough love for myself to stop being so hard on myself." This will help you to accept yourself for who you are and take better care of yourself by letting go of self-pity. Repeat it when times get tough, until it starts to sink in.

6. If you're feeling self-pity, try to redirect your thoughts to something positive. Focus on all the good things in your life, whether it's the people you love or your favorite hobby or sport. It will help ease the negative feelings that tend to come with self-pity, making it easier for you to feel better about yourself.

7. Take things one day at a time. Don't worry about what you have to do tomorrow or the day after tomorrow. Worrying will only make you feel more anxious. Accept your feelings and remember that everything is going to be okay, as long as you put your feelings into words and speak to someone who will help change the way you think about yourself.

8. Be your own best friend and be kind to yourself when times get tough. Take time for yourself and do something you like. It might be reading a book, listening to music, or doing something outdoors. This will make you feel better about yourself and will

help you to forgive yourself when you make mistakes.

9. Express your feelings in a constructive way and be true to yourself when things don't go according to plan. Don't hide in a shell and let your insecurities and failures make you feel like a failure. Remember to be patient and stay true to the person you really are.

10. Write down your thoughts, feelings and concerns in a journal. This will give you an opportunity to express yourself and let go of the negative side of your personality when it gets too much for you. You can read through the old writings and remind yourself that everything is going to be okay, as long as you don't dwell on it.

11. Tell someone how you feel about them or a specific situation regarding you that's bothering you. This will help you feel better about yourself and get rid of your negative feelings. It will also show them how there is someone who cares about making sure their feelings are taken care of and that they are able to be happy.

12. When overwhelmed with negative feelings, stay busy doing something fun or develop a hobby. This will allow you to focus on other things and keep your mind off your problems and weaknesses. It will also allow you to appreciate the things that make you

who you are and help you to focus on making your life better, instead of wallowing in self-pity.

13. Don't worry about yesterday or tomorrow because they constantly change, making it futile to dwell on them. In fact, yesterday and tomorrow don't even physically exist. Much of the time we spend getting upset over them is, therefore, energy spent on things that have no reality. It's a waste of time and will only bring negativity into your life. Worrying about what happened yesterday means our thoughts are constantly filled with negativity. All that does is make us feel worse about ourselves instead of better.

14. Think of yourself as a work in progress. People aren't perfect and neither are you. Recognize that you are always improving your weaknesses and learn to accept that everyone has their flaws. Nobody is perfect but try to focus on your strengths more than your weaknesses.

15. Don't compare yourself to others, when trying to feel better about yourself. It will only make you unhappy when you don't measure up to others or achieve what they have achieved or done in life.

FORGIVING YOURSELF AND OTHERS

"Forget your past, forgive yourself, and begin again."

— ANONYMOUS

Forgive and forget is common advice that is easier said than done for most of us. Some people find it easier to forgive others but not themselves. Others might have been victims of bullying, crime, or abuse. When the hurt runs deep, our trust is shattered, and our inner world might be in turmoil, disrupting our life and relationships. The path of forgiveness is to heal your inner world by addressing the pain that is stopping you from living your best life.

Here are some points to think about:

Remember, forgiveness is a choice you have to make.

There is a difference between forgive and forget. Forgetting means you forgot the past incidents, but it doesn't mean you forgave the people involved. If you still hold bitterness inside toward that situation or person, those buried feelings may still cause you problems and unhappiness.

Forgiveness takes time, and especially so when the consequences are devastating.

Forgiveness does not mean you condone the behavior or what happened.

Completely forgetting the past is impossible. Instead, accept reality for what it is. You can help yourself, by asking why and how it happened or take responsibility for your actions, if any.

If you want to forgive others, it helps to hear their side and talk to them before passing judgment.

Even if you are not satisfied with the outcome of the talk or can't reach out to the person involved - learn to move on and accept it for what it is.

You don't necessarily need to reconcile with the person. You just want to release the past.

If you are asking forgiveness from others, it helps to make amends to those you have wronged. You can try talking and explaining to them why you did those things, e.g., bullying.

Learn to forgive yourself first. Once you have forgiven yourself, you will find it easier to accept forgiveness from others or to forgive others for any wrongdoing.

Accept your imperfections and know that humans make mistakes. If you made a mistake - correct your actions and ask for forgiveness. It will help you to stop thinking negatively or using your mistakes as an excuse to not move forward.

Forgiveness means letting go of the flaws in your life.

Forgiveness means making peace with your family, friends, and other people.

It is not what happened ten years ago that is hurting you, but your reaction to it whenever you think of the offense. Your responses in the here and now to something that probably no longer exists is the real problem. That's the mental and emotional habit you have to let go.

Benefits of Forgiveness

It helps you to remove the mental block to your self-progress and success in life.

Allows you to release negative emotions, e.g., hate, bitterness, and anger that are trapped inside your body and mind.

It will help you to find joy and see the real meaning in contentment and happiness.

You will be more carefree, not worrying about any wrongdoings.

Your mindset will become more positive.

You can now focus fully on your goals rather than dwelling on the past.

You can live your life with fewer heartaches.

Suggestion on forgiving others:

1. Express to them about how their actions hurt you. If this person is no longer in your life or you do not want to see them, you can just write a letter, burn it, and move on. If you want to maintain a relationship with this person, tell them your feelings in a non-aggressive manner. Either way, putting your feelings into words will help you to let go.

2. Journaling is a safe place to express your emotions and feelings. You can write about what happened and how you feel. You can try to look for the positive growth that comes out of it. Keep writing until you find it easier to move on.

3. Cultivate empathy and see if you can try to understand their actions and motives. For example, your mother was raised by strict parents, so she did not know how to show you much affection and was very critical. Remember, empathy does not mean you agree with what they did to you, but it can help you to work toward forgiveness and understand that all humans are flawed.

4. You can forgive the other person without telling them or including them in your life.

5. Forgiving is for your benefit, not theirs. The other person doesn't even have to know that you have forgiven them. It is about putting the final seal on the past that hurt you.

Suggestions on self-forgiveness:

1. Acknowledge your emotions and know that this process will require you to have understanding, compassion, kindness, and empathy toward yourself.

2. It gives a voice to your thoughts and emotions, by saying it out loud or writing it down. It helps to relieve the burden you are carrying.

3. Reframe by thinking of your mistake as a lesson learned or experience to help you be better next time.

4. If you can't put the matter out of your mind, put it on hold by imagining a container, e.g., a mason jar or box where you put this matter inside for now. You can return to it later when you feel you're ready.

5. You may find your inner critic giving you a hard time. You can consider journaling to:

- Write out a conversation.
- Write a compassionate answer to each negative thing your inner critic says.
- Identify negative thought patterns.
- Make a list of your positive qualities and strengths.

6. If your mistake involves hurting someone, consider if you can apologize or make amends.

7. Replaying your mistake and feeling bad is not going to help. Try to refocus your attention on something positive e.g., go for a walk or help out at the animal shelter or soup kitchen.

8. Be patient and know that it can take days or years. You can't rush the process, especially when it involves emotions and feelings. Give yourself space and time to let go.

9. Honor your imperfections.

Remember, there is no one-size-fits-all solution, when it comes to forgiveness. With some self-compassion, you can move past what cannot be undone and get on with your life unburdened by past events.

Chapter Summary

The main focus of this chapter was; Understanding the difference between self-compassion and self-pity to avoid falling into the trap.

- Self-Pity or Being Compassionate
- Mindfulness and Compassion
- Mindfulness beyond Meditation
- Self-Pity
- Forgiving Yourself and Others
- Benefits of Forgiveness

In the next chapter, you will learn; Best Practices for Nurturing Your Inner Child.

8

BEST PRACTICES FOR
NURTURING YOUR INNER CHILD

Focus: More strategies and techniques for loving your inner child, keeping your relationships intact, and maintaining your success for as long as you want.

F ew people realize that to heal from traumatic childhood experiences, it's often necessary to treat our inner child. Our inner child is the part of us which was alive and developing before our personality and sense of self were fully formed. It's the essential part of us that must be treated to get the best results. When we treat our inner child, that important part of us, we can heal old wounds and trauma that has held that part of us hostage throughout our entire life. We human beings have two parts to our being - a conscious mind and a subconscious mind. Our conscious mind is what most people think about most of the time. The subconscious mind is the part of us that is living while we are asleep, dreaming while we are awake, and at work while we are sleeping. The subconscious mind is the creative part of us that sparks all our creative ideas, schemes, schemas, creativity, etc.

Many people mistake their conscious minds for their whole being. They think they are creative because they have creative ideas in their conscious minds. However, creative ideas in their conscious minds are only a fraction of who they really are. They do not have a conscious image of their true selves. The majority of their being does not have a sense of self at all. The way to treat our inner child is to start treating the subconscious mind that is hiding from us. Doing this will help us heal from our childhood wounds. We need to know how to love and accept ourselves, if we are going to heal from the traumas in our lives. Our inner child accepts us unconditionally. It's not the same as the unconscious mind that often holds us hostage. Once we love and accept ourselves, then our inner child is liberated. It can then begin to help us heal from the traumas that caused us to suppress it in the first place. Why do we need to treat our inner child? Because children learn from their experiences what they will become as adults.

COMMUNICATE WITH YOUR INNER HEART

It's imperative that you begin allowing your inner child to express themself rather than continuing to repress the powerful emotions. You can do this by:

Addressing any father and/or mother wounds from the past through your journaling. Write your mom or dad a letter (don't worry - you won't be sending it) and let them know what you needed from them but never received. This can help to relieve the pressure in your heart immensely!

Journal another letter addressed to your inner child, the wounded place in you, but this time use the three personality egos to talk to them: the child, the adult, and the parent.

Don't stop at one letter. For those of us with significant emotional pain, it may take several different letters to get everything released.

DESIGN SELF-CARE ACTIVITIES

You need to determine whether your need for each of the following is met:

1. Need for Friendship

In order to meet this need, you need to be around other like-minded people to make new friends. They don't have to be the "popular" crew. People with too many "friends" are often very shallow and vain. Join an organization, group, or club with people with whom you share similar interests. You can take advantage of social websites like Twitter or Facebook to meet new people. Joining a team, such as a sports team, band, or choir with a laid-back attitude and no competitive mindset can also be a great way to make friends.

2. Need for Respect

If you're looking to get respect, first ensure that you respect others. Try not to badmouth other people, especially not if you're doing it to make you feel better about yourself by feeling superior to them. If there's enough of a problem with someone, try addressing the issue directly rather than talking about them behind their backs. Also ensure that you're demonstrating respect for yourself. Take care of your appearance, exercise, and have good hygiene. Ask yourself if you enjoy your own company.

3. Need for Affection

Everyone needs affection. One good way to enjoy affection is via a pet, such as a cat or a dog. Pets offer us unconditional love. However, be careful: nothing should be seen as the source of your happiness. That's always you. You can also find a good friend, mate, or companion to participate in any available free hugs campaigns around you. You can also create your own, if you dare to be outgoing enough. In addition, you could join an online community that you feel comfortable about and make friends on the web that you may one day meet in person.

Be careful not to become dependent, a person who relies on someone else for emotional stability. If you feel your mind is attached to an animal or a person for your happiness, you must start rewiring your thinking all over again. Always remember that you are the source of controlling the way you feel about anything, whether happy or sad.

4. Need for a Supreme Being

If you are interested in spiritual matters, there is no better way to find inner peace than setting aside the time for prayer or meditation, regardless of your religious affiliation.

5. Need for a Creative Expression

Children appreciate and have fun learning and developing new skills, such as coloring, painting, writing, arts and crafts, and making music. This is a great way to express your thoughts and feelings. To develop creative expression, it's vital that you avoid taking yourself too seriously. Look for a place that will inspire you and help you rekindle your creativity, such as a quiet and peaceful spot like the outdoors or a bright and colorful place that makes you feel artistic. Don't be shy about trying new things. If you want to have a go at sculpting, who's stopping you? You can always try something else if you find it's not for you after all!

6. Need for Play and Fun

Life is short; no one gets out alive, right? In order to include more fun and play in your life to improve your self-esteem, you need to reinvent yourself. Change your routine! Schedule some movies, walks, dances, massages, or music in your life.

7. Need for Serving Others

Being of service to others in need can be a source of joy for you and those you help out. And it doesn't have to be much. You can volunteer at hospitals, social service agencies, or shelters, by offering your services to those in need. In addition, it doesn't hurt to do something unexpected or random. It can be as simple as sending an e-mail to a friend or family member, telling him or her why you appreciate them. Send something honest, from the heart.

8. Need for Intimacy

Being intimate isn't all about sex; it's so much more. Simple acts like breathing together can be extremely intimate and romantic. Even holding hands and having a nap on your partner's lap can be relaxing and comforting. It's all about being more vulnerable with other people.

WRITE A LETTER OF SUPPORT TO YOURSELF

Be sure to address each of the following when you are expressing your inner child:

- Pain
- Anger
- Regret
- Fear
- Desire
- Intent

As you write, if you're right-handed, try using your left hand and vice versa. This often helps bring back your childhood feelings and state of mind, which is very helpful to this process.

SURROUND YOURSELF WITH POSITIVE, SUPPORTIVE, AND ENCOURAGING PEOPLE

Being around negative people can obviously have a negative effect on you. On the other hand, surrounding yourself with positive people can create the nurturing atmosphere you need for healing your heart's wounds. The key to healing emotional disturbances is to concentrate on observing your moods. Are they more negative or positive in most situations? Evaluate those around you, the people in your life, be it casual, personal, or professional. Avoid getting into situations where you have to deal with toxic or overly negative people. Be sure to seek out team members, friendships, relationships, and even companionship with people who welcome every obstacle in their way as a challenge, rather than something that drives them into anxiety and fear.

READ, LISTEN TO, AND WATCH PERSONAL GROWTH MATERIAL

Lifting your self-esteem is all about learning to be naturally positive and developing a positive energy around you. You don't have to manufacture your unhappiness. It's all about getting to the other side of the coin. You can increase your positivity, by immersing yourself in personal growth material, such as positive magazines, other self-help books, and motivational television programs.

PRACTICE RECEIVING APPROVAL FROM YOURSELF RATHER THAN OTHERS

Create a list of people your mind believes you need approval from and explore this need through your journaling. The need for approval from others greatly affects your healing time. These phantom concerns can cause you to neglect doing important things, make you procrastinate, and experience unnecessary fear and anxiety. To start feeling better, you need to make a decision, not for others, but for yourself. As you see the nothingness of these beliefs, you strengthen your sense of self-acceptance in such a way that you no longer need to look for approval from others in anything that you do. You may seek advice or counsel from those you respect, but the inherent sense of insecurity will no longer be there.

BECOME KNOWLEDGEABLE OR SKILLED

Develop and grow in one subject or area that you enjoy. It could be sports, music, politics, nutrition, social concerns, art, gardening, history, spirituality, parenting, cooking, or culture. The greater your skillset and capabilities, the more of your True Self you're drawing on to sustain them, which creates a naturally healthy self-esteem.

Stress

It's very important to eliminate as much stress from your daily experience as possible. For those with stressful or high-tension jobs, finding ways to manage stress well is key to this inner work. Uncontrolled stress can be a significant inhibitor to your ability to unleash the inner child that's hurting within you. Understanding the kind of personality that's subject to stress can help us to discover exactly what works best in healing the emotional pain. Take a look at the following stress personalities to determine who you are, in whole or in part.

- **The Warrior:** Mentally wringing hands with a tendency to see things getting worse with negative 'what if' statements.
- **The Perfectionist:** You tend to believe that you never do enough and need to work harder or do better. There's often a fear of looking bad or of someone finding fault with you or the work you've done.
- **The Critic:** You're always judging yourself negatively, concentrating more on your weaknesses and suppressing or even refusing to recognize your strengths.
- **The Victim:** You feel hopeless, helpless, and you're

full of despair about the future. You habitually think things like: "I'll never stop feeling this way," or "Things will never change for me..."

Ask Yourself these Questions for All Types:

- What is the evidence that supports my pattern of thinking?
- Is it always true or am I just used to believing it?
- What are the odds I can see things differently?
- What's the big picture?

Journal your responses and review your answers later. Wash, rinse, repeat. You will eventually discover that some of the fears that have lowered your self-esteem are actually completely unfounded.

PARENTING THE INNER CHILD

The child that you once were is still inside you. However, you are no longer a child anymore. You're an adult now, and to heal your Inner Child, you must become your own parent. Even if the trauma in your childhood came from adults or situations other than your parents, the psychological wounds you sustained were not healed. The child did not get the love and support that it needed in order to grow in a natural and healthy way. To discover your Inner Child, you need to reach out to yourself the way a parent might reach out to a hurting child.

There are some practical tools that you can use to re-parent your Inner Child, but there are some emotional tools that you will also need. The first is Love. Every time and every way that you approach your Inner Child, it must come from a place of love. Harshness, cruelty, and criticism won't work. These are the very things that your Inner Child is firmly insulated against. The traumatic dynamics that caused your Inner Child to retreat can be difficult to shed, especially at first. If you were parented by people who were critical, abusive, or neglectful, this is your primary model for what parenting is. Therefore, this parenting style will feel the most familiar to you, even if you recognize how harmful it is. For this reason, the second emotional tool you need is Patience. Healing doesn't happen overnight. It doesn't always happen in the way that you want or expect. Be patient with yourself. Allow yourself to be vulnerable, both as a parent and child. Allow yourself to make mistakes, to progress slowly and slowly avoid regressing. Trust that you are on the right path and respect your journey.

The final emotional tool that you need is forgiveness. Traumatic experiences are often humiliating, and our responses to them are to blame ourselves for their happening. You may have done things as a child that you are ashamed or embarrassed about. You may have done some things as an adult that were hurtful, cruel, or shameful. Trauma is frequently derived from external sources. There will be people in your past who inflicted the wounds that you are now trying to heal. Forgiving people who have hurt you does not mean validating, excusing, or justifying their behavior. Forgiveness is about acceptance. In order to heal the wounds of the traumatic past, you must let go of the anger, hatred, or resentment you are currently holding toward the people that hurt you. It doesn't mean that what was done to you was okay. It means that you are ready to reclaim control over your own happiness. By carrying anger and hatred inside you, you are allowing that person to repeatedly hurt you and your Inner Child.

Re-parenting Tools and Strategies

In addition to your three emotional tools (Love, Patience, and Forgiveness), there are many different activities and exercises you can do to reach out to your Inner Child and open up opportunities for re-parenting. Everyone's mind and body work differently. Therefore, not every activity will feel right for you. Inner Child Healing is a journey, on which you will undergo some dramatic transformations. Who you are one day may be very different from the person you are the next day. If an exercise or activity isn't working for you now, let it go. When you're ready, you can always go back to it.

Most of the re-parenting exercises in this book are spiritual, physical, and emotional. They are rooted in the arts, meditation, mindfulness, and fitness. Medication is not recommended. If you feel like medication is something that you need, speak with a psychiatrist or physician that you trust. Psychiatric medication is something you should never feel embarrassed or ashamed to take. However, it rarely solves the problem by itself. If you want to take or are currently on medication, use your meds the way mechanics use jacks when they work on cars. The jack props up the car and holds it firmly in place, so that the mechanic can safely see what's going on and do the necessary repair work. Psych meds are jacks for your emotions, propping them up and holding them in place, so that you can safely do the work you need to without getting crushed.

Drawing

Drawing and other forms of visual art can be an amazingly powerful tool for Inner Child Healing. Drawing, painting and playing with clay are things that children do spontaneously, happily, and naturally. We only lose our artistic inclinations as adults, when we are made to feel ashamed of something that we've created. Drawing is so ingrained in our natural human development that it comes well before writing. Art therapy is often used with children who refuse to speak or who feel they cannot verbalize their feelings. Inviting your Inner Child to color and draw can give you the freedom to finally say things you were never able to put into words. If you are artistically inclined as an adult, you know that the process of creating visual art breaks you out of rational, analytical mental states. If you suffered with very restrictive parents or an education that prioritized verbal logic, drawing can help you reconnect with your natural, childlike creative impulses. Everyone is capable of making art. It's a natural, necessary part of our development. The stifling of creativity through shame or criticism leaves very real wounds on the Inner Child. Drawing through our self-doubts and self-criticisms allows us to speak with the Inner Child in its own language.

Writing

Language is an integral part of our experience as humans. Though we tend to associate writing with the intellect, language is deeply emotionally and culturally coded. Certain words and phrases can sometimes trigger deep emotional responses within us. Poets have known this for centuries as have novelists, songwriters, and playwrights. Screenwriters in Hollywood know this. Bloggers, lawyers, and politicians know this. For this reason, journaling can be an extremely effective tool for re-parenting and reaching out to our wounded Inner Child. An effective strategy is to set up a two-way journal. One side is written from you, the parent, to your Inner Child. The other is written from you, the Child, to the re-parenting adult self. Writing these letters to yourself (or to other people in your life, if that feels right and natural for you to do) allows your Inner Child to finally speak in a safe, supportive space to an adult that it can trust.

Meditation

Stillness is also an action that we often forget we can take. Did you daydream a lot as a child? Guided imagery meditation is daydreaming with a purpose. It involves intentionally conjuring up a series of imagined images, conversations, landscapes, or scenes that ultimately help us to release feelings of anger and pain. After a heated argument, do you ever lay in bed imagining all the things you should have said? Before a date, do you imagine what it's going to be like in your head? Guided imagery meditations are like healing fantasies that give us the same kind of emotional release, but in a much more targeted and productive way. In meditation, you and your Inner Child can be together in the same space. You can hug, play, talk, laugh, and cry, all the things that parents do with their children to foster feelings of love, security, and harmony.

WORKING WITH YOUR FEELINGS

When a family is dysfunctional, the needs of the child are not met. When we are little, not getting our needs met is incredibly painful. That pain is compounded when the adults in our lives are unable or unwilling to listen to, support, or nurture us. When we repeatedly find ourselves in this situation, we start to develop coping mechanisms that allow us to defend against our feelings. Shutting out our feelings allows us to survive as children, but we grow into adults that are strangers to our likes and dislikes, hopes and dreams, fears and ambitions. When you have a wounded Inner Child, you must learn again how to experience your feelings. A three-step process is described below to help you to reconnect with your emotions and learn to feel and share them in a healthy, authentic way.

1. **Identifying your Feelings:** Sometimes, the wounds to the Inner Child are so severe that we shut ourselves off from our emotions altogether. We are afraid to feel anything at all because expressing authentic feelings requires a certain level of vulnerability. If you are at this level of awareness with your feelings, then you need to start small. Simply focus on naming and owning your emotions. Get a "feelings chart" off the Internet (a simple Google search of "feelings chart" will yield hundreds of results, so choose the one you like the most). At the end of every day, take a look at your chart. Record in your journal which feelings you felt that day and when. If you felt happy, what made you feel that way? If you felt sad, why? How did you handle those feelings? Slowly but surely, you will become more and more comfortable with your feelings. You'll be able to recognize your emotions without the aid of your chart, and you'll have a new language of emotion to help you share your feelings authentically with other people in your life.

2. **Sharing Your Feelings:** Sharing your feelings is a

fundamental part of achieving intimacy with other people. When our Inner Child is wounded, however, we learn to be very careful about how we express our feelings. People who grow up in dysfunctional families are often punished for being vulnerable or authentic and find it difficult to trust other people with their true feelings. This dynamic separates us from our true selves and causes us to be manipulative or emotionally distant, sometimes without even realizing it. If you are at this level of awareness with your feelings, then the tool you need to heal is trust. Slowly but surely, practice opening up to people that you consider close to you. Maybe that person is a family member, a friend, a partner, even a co-worker. Go slow and go easy. People who have trouble expressing their feelings often "share" their feelings as ideas or opinions rather than expressing them for what they are. To circumvent this, challenge yourself to use one "I feel" statement every day. Again, make sure to say it to someone you trust, not just anyone. If you keep at it, eventually, it won't be a challenge anymore. Each time your honesty, authenticity, and intimacy are rewarded rather than punished, accepted rather than judged, another wall around your Inner Child is torn down.

3. **Exposing your Feelings:** At this third level of feelings awareness, you can recognize and honestly express your feelings. However, you may find

202 | DON BARLOW

yourself retreating or shutting down when someone else responds in kind. You may find yourself only sharing what you know will be accepted and hiding what you think will be rejected. This level of awareness is only semi-functional. It certainly won't serve you to share everything that pops into your head at every moment (this, too, is dysfunctional in its own way). However, if you find yourself keeping secrets from people you are close to, this, too, can be a sign of a wounded Inner Child. It's one thing to draw healthy boundaries around your personal and public life. It's something altogether different to purposely mislead someone because you are afraid that telling the truth and being authentic will lead to negative consequences. Every person makes mistakes, but in order to have healthy, loving relationships, we must own up to those mistakes. A true friend will never reject you for being honest. A loving partner will never belittle you for admitting to something you are ashamed of. If you are at this level, you must learn to expose yourself to potential conflict.

We often justify manipulative behavior, by pretending that we are protecting the other person - "I don't want her to get hurt," you might say, or "I just don't think it's worth the argument," convincing yourself or others that you are being the bigger person and taking the high road by staying silent.

This is not authentic behavior. It is not being honest with yourself. Children can be startlingly direct and won't hesitate to share their feelings honestly, with no fear of the social consequences. It's to this childlike acceptance of the validity of your own feelings that you must return to. Did you keep a "Secret Diary" as a child? It's time to make one again. Commit to fifteen minutes every night before you go to bed, or even ten if this feels like more than you can spare. In your Secret Diary, on one side, write down anything that you wanted to say to someone that day but didn't. Write down what you said to that person instead of the truth and why. Then, on the other side, write down what you could have said to that person that would have expressed the truth.

As an example, we'll use the classic "Does this dress make me look fat?" question. In this situation, you are withholding a thought rather than a feeling. However, the basic idea is the same. In your secret diary, write down that your partner asked you this question. Write what you wanted to say and write what you actually said. Maybe you wanted to say, "Yes, you look huge!" but you said, "No darling, you look gorgeous." Maybe your partner felt happy and supported, but would it not have been more supportive to be honest and help your partner find a dress that really looks good on them? On the other side of the page, think about what you could have said. "You look huge!" may not be appropriate, but what about "Honestly, it doesn't flatter you at all. Maybe try a different color?" Or "Yes, but what's wrong with that? I think it looks great!" Or "I don't want to hurt you, but yes, that dress is not doing you any favors." There are ways to be true to ourselves without hurting others. After a while, you won't need your secret diary anymore. You'll have trained yourself to speak authentically and honestly right there in the moment, and you'll be amazed at how much the quality of your relationships improves.

HEARING YOUR INNER CHILD

If your Inner Child is wounded, you may have become very good at silencing it. As you begin your journey of healing, it can be difficult to distinguish which of your Inner Voices is the voice of your False, Defensive Self and which is the voice of the True Self or the Inner Child. To help yourself hear your Inner Child, listen more carefully to your inner conversations. Make note of every time one of your thoughts begins with something like "I should...," "I have to...," or "I need to..." This kind of inner speech is not coming from a nurturing place; it's coming from a place of control. Every time you start speaking to yourself this way, you are bullying and silencing the Inner Child. Children rarely pressure themselves in this way because this kind of language robs the recipient of agency. If you have to or need to do something, you don't have a choice. If you should (or should not) do something, there is a judgment being made. Again, you lose agency. Strict parents often use this kind of language. If you grew up with strict parents, then you will probably find yourself using this kind of language when you are parenting yourself. However, this is not the voice of the authentic self. The voice that responds to those controlling thoughts is the voice of the Inner Child.

BUILDING RESILIENCY

Deep Breathing Exercises

When we feel strong emotions of any kind, our breathing becomes heavy and erratic. However, the opposite is also true. If our breathing is heavy and erratic, it's very hard for us to relax. When you are doing any healing work with your Inner Child, it is important to be aware of breathing. Strong emotions can and will well up from within you. Childhood trauma is something that we bury for a reason. Breathing slowly, deeply, and mindfully brings our thoughts back to our breath, and, therefore, back to our body. Whenever we feel angry, sad, or frightened, returning you to your body will return you to the present moment. The danger is gone, but your feelings can be as intense as they were in the moment of crisis. Bringing yourself back to the body brings you back from the past moment of trauma to the present moment of peace and gives you the stability you need to transform from frightened child to comforting parent. Breathing mindfully keeps you in a tranquil physical space, so that you can ask the Inner Child what is wrong, confront the wrongs you may have done as a child or an adult, and approach the conflicts you're having within yourself or out in the world with love, patience, and forgiveness.

Releasing Trapped Feelings

The feelings and events that most often accompany trauma and leave the biggest scars on the Inner Child are: anger, guilt, shame, grief, abandonment, rejection, neglect, powerlessness, hopelessness, and feeling trapped or worthless. To heal the Inner Child, these feelings must be released. To do this, we must develop resiliency.

People who have experienced trauma respond in one of two ways: submit or rebound. When we submit to a traumatic experience, we essentially agree with the perpetrator. We believe that we, in some way, deserved what happened to us. As adults, this often presents as codependency. When your long-distance partner forgets to call you, you may feel angry and then guilty for being angry. When your parents say something that humiliates or disrespects you, you hide your hurt and pretend to laugh it off. When we do this, we are not allowing ourselves to experience our feelings authentically. We are disconnected from the Inner Child. The first reaction is a spontaneous age regression. Your Inner Child throws up its defenses, so that it doesn't have to feel the pain of rejection. Resiliency is the ability to grow out of difficult or trying situations. It's not about being stoic or invincible. It's not about never having any negative feelings. It's about choosing to acknowledge negative feelings without judgment and releasing them in authentic, harmonious ways. Resiliency is the inevitable result of a happy, whole Inner Child. When we have successfully healed the traumatic wounds of the past, we are better able to face future problems with strength, courage, and compassion.

MAKING YOUR INNER CHILD FEEL SAFE

"When I'm with you, I feel safe from the things that hurt me inside."

— ANONYMOUS

The next step after befriending your inner child is to develop trust. Your inner child needs to know that he or she can trust you and that you are here to nurture and protect it. To achieve this, your inner child needs to feel safe as they do not want to be hurt again. Some psychotherapists call this process 're-parenting,' where you now play the role of a responsible, concerned, and trustworthy parent to your inner child.

We have already established that many of our adult problems in life, such as not being able to have meaningful relationships or self-sabotaging inclinations, are a result of our inner child growing up feeling insecure and unloved because their needs were never met. Even though you try to ignore your inner child, he or she never leaves and instead resides in your subconscious mind - influencing how you live your life, make decisions, or respond to difficulties. However, by making your inner child feel safe again, you can now make peace with the past and repair negative patterns in your life.

Ways to make your inner child feel safe:

1. Affirmations

Positive affirmations can help you change old beliefs. It is a good way to begin by reaffirming your inner child with words of love and healing. You can say affirmations any time you want, and you can say them to yourself by looking in the mirror.

Suggestions:

Acknowledge their feelings

If you have a habit of suppressing your feelings and trying to act brave, then it's possible you were discouraged from crying or expressing yourself as a child. However, those pent-up feelings that weren't allowed to come out may fester inside you as an adult. They can impact the way you behave and the choices you make. Tell your inner child today, "I hear you. You are safe to be yourself. Everything is going to be alright." You have now finally given a voice to all the hurt and pain you suppressed.

Love

Many of us had parents who didn't tell us we deserved to be loved. It may not have been their fault. Many parents, especially from older generations, were not encouraged to be demonstrative. In fact, some parents may even think that showing love and affection weakens a child. So, tell your inner child that they are loved. You can say, "I love you just the way you are. You are always safe and protected. "

Apologize

Children often do not know better and think they deserve to be criticized, shamed, abused, or abandoned. They tell themselves they did something wrong to deserve it. Your inner child is always pure and innocent. It is time for you to rectify this, by apologizing to your inner child for all the past hurts. You can say, "I am sorry. You deserve to be safe and protected from now onward."

Thank you

Despite everything that has happened to you in the past, you are here today because your inner child never gave up. Together both of you have got past the rough moments and persevered. You can say, "Thank you for not giving up. You are safe and supported all the time," or "Thank you for doing your best. You are safe and protected - now and always."

2. **Routines**

Time equals security. Therefore, establish a familiar routine with your inner child where you are constantly checking in through talking, sharing, and learning together. Routines help to form a secure attachment with your inner child because you are creating a consistent and predictable place for them to see you as constant security in all aspects of their lives.

3. **Praises**

Take time to praise your inner child. It's a way of rebuilding its self-worth and self-esteem. Your verbal encouragement gives your inner child the security it needs to blossom. For example, "Good idea. You are good at spontaneity. You are always safe to tell me anything."

4. **Listen**

After ignoring your inner child for so many years, they probably have a lot to say to you. Like typical children, they throw tantrums and act out when they can't express their frustrations. Whenever your inner child wants to speak, make sure that you are all ears. Through listening, you can learn so much about your inner child. You will also build trust with your inner child, as they will feel safe talking to you about anything under the sun.

5. **Don't hold back the love**

Show your inner child in small gestures every day that you care. It can be saying encouraging words, being available and open, or just having their back if they feel unsafe, threatened, or vulnerable.

6. Let them be who they are

Your inner child has his or her own set of unique characteristics. Accept them in each moment, even the difficult times of angry outbursts and overwhelming emotions. By accepting who your inner child is, you are validating their emotions and showing them that it is safe to be who they are with you. Once your inner child senses this, they will feel safe and comfortable in your presence. All the past hurts, fears, and insecurities might have gotten the better of your inner child. However, you are here now to create a new environment of safety, security, and trust through your words, actions, and everyday living.

EMBRACING THE FUN IN LIFE

Reconnecting with your inner child can be an incredibly rewarding experience. This new perspective in life will lead you to finding happiness in the things you used to overlook. You slowly regain trust in yourself and in the hopes and dreams that you had long since forgotten. You learn to love and appreciate yourself and others again. Indeed, life holds much more pleasure, once you reawaken your inner child.

Healthy Habits you can Learn from the Inner Child

Your inner child will lead you to experience the fun part of life. This will make you a happier and more balanced individual. Learn to nurture a childlike spirit within you, and you will be able to live your life to the fullest with much less strife. Compare that with an adulthood where all you have is seriousness and frustrations.

Stop holding yourself back too much. Children are impulsive and curious. They like to indulge in as much enjoyment as possible and think of the consequences later. While there is much sense in delaying gratification or treading carefully, it is also healthy to let go and not restrict yourself too much every once in a while. After all, new experiences and ideas can be refreshing.

Let go of your worries. Children are naturally carefree. Their concerns revolve around the simplest things, such as whether dinner's going to taste good or if Santa Claus will indeed give them what they want for Christmas. Their feelings border on excitement more than worry. Worrying too much when something is beyond your control, is not going to do you any good. Whenever you catch yourself fretting over something, take a deep breath and have fun. Play a game or watch a fun movie. Take your mind off serious things and let time pass; everything will turn out right.

Engage all of your senses. Children are always amazed by the new things they discover in this world. Bring this feeling back to life, by soaking up the world with your senses: sight, smell, touch, taste, and hearing. Do you like the fresh bouquet of flowers your spouse sent to you? Inhale their delicious scent, enjoy the bright colors, and touch the silken petals.

Don't hold grudges. Children often let go of bad feelings after a while, and they will go back to their cheerful and loving selves because they prefer to forget unhappy thoughts. You can also adapt this. Let your inner child forgive and forget all of those who have hurt you in the past and just look forward to a brighter future. If someone has hurt your feelings, go ahead and cry it out, then wipe your tears, eat some ice cream, watch a funny movie and go out with your friends. You know that life's too short and fun to stay mad forever.

Having Fun with Your Inner Child

Embracing the fun in life is entirely different for the inner child. You do not need to go jet-setting to some foreign location or spend a lot of money on expensive items to experience joy. The inner child is delighted by the simplest things in life. To evoke the inner child's version of embracing life, you can try out the following suggestions and, along the way, discover so much more on your own as well.

Visit the Toy Store or the Candy Store. Do you remember loving these places when you were a kid? You would look forward to your parents bringing you there, so that you could look around and drink up all of the colors, shapes, and amazing new-fangled thingamajigs and treats that made your imagination go wild! Go ahead and look around the store, see if you can find anything that makes you feel delighted, entertained, or even nostalgic. If you don't mind, don't overthink, and just buy it for your inner child to have fun with.

Play with kids. Let kids awaken the inner child in you by immersing yourself in their world. Visit a relatives' kids or offer to babysit them for a day. Adults usually worry too much about the kids being noisy and messy. However, it is better to let go of all those thoughts and just have fun with them. Go to a swimming pool and play, or run around the park, blow bubbles, and then enjoy a picnic of sticky food. If they are girls, you can have a tea party with them, while watching Disney's "Alice in Wonderland", jump rope, or make paper dolls. Let loose your inner child with real play-mates. Just make sure to hold on to the responsible adult side of you, and that is to protect them from any danger.

Drink up the feeling of excitement. Children don't really care too much about what other people think when they're having fun. Sometimes they scream and shout because they are so filled with elation that they could just burst. You can also try that. For instance, if you are on top of a mountain, you can just scream your lungs out. If you are playing with your friends, shriek in delight when they catch you in a game of tag. Run around the yard with your dog and actually pretend that he's the Abominable Snowman while he's chasing you. Plan a surprise for a friend and feel giddy with anticipation. Visit a carnival and don't hold back the lively feeling when you are about to hop on a ride, then shout as loud as you can as the roller coaster whirls you around.

Read Fairy Tales and Books about Magic. Children love listening to someone read to them stories of kings, queens, princesses, knights in shining armor, pirates, lost treasure, elves and fairies, witches, and wizards. Plunge into this magical world of books and let your inner child escape to different places and times.

Throw a kiddie party. Kids love parties filled with games, cake, ice cream, and presents. If you have an upcoming celebration such as a birthday or a reunion, why not make it a kiddie party-themed gathering? Hang fliers, blow up balloons, get a big and colorful cake, and prepare fun giveaways filled with candies and toys.

Eat a treat. Kids don't count calories. They simply indulge. Of course, their metabolism is skyrocketing. Therefore, they are usually safe to do that, you might be thinking. However, you don't have to eat a treat on a daily basis. It's good to indulge in some brownies or cookies or chocolate fudge every once in a while. Think of nothing else in the world, except how scrumptious it is.

Allowing your inner child to embrace the fun in life does not mean that you will let go of your responsibilities of being an adult. However, when everything seems too dull or dreary to bear, then it is time to loosen up and let your inner child take reign.

Chapter Summary

The main focus of this chapter was: more strategies and techniques for loving your inner child, keeping your relationships intact, and maintaining your success for as long as you want.

- Communicate with Your Inner Heart
- Design Self-Care Activities
- Write A Letter of Support to Yourself
- Surround Yourself with Positive, Supportive, and Encouraging People
- Read, Listen, And Watch Personal Growth Material
- Practice Receiving Approval from Yourself Rather than Others
- Become Knowledgeable or Skilled
- Parenting the Inner Child
- Re-parenting Tools and Strategies
- Working with Your Feelings
- Hearing your Inner Child
- Building Resiliency
- Deep Breathing Exercises
- Releasing Trapped Feelings
- Making Your Inner Child Feel Safe
- Ways to Make Your Inner Child Feel Safe
- Embracing the Fun in Life
- Healthy Habits You Can Learn From the Inner Child
- Having Fun with Your Inner Child

FINAL WORDS

Childhood is not simply a transition into adulthood. From the moment we are born, we are fully realized beings capable of complex interactions with the world around us. There are a series of experiences that every human must have in order to develop into a fully mature adult. Trauma, however, can redirect childhood growth or stop it altogether. Adulthood is not about years of life; it's about richness of experience. Most humans have wounds of one kind or another to their Inner Child. Most adults are able to function happily and healthily in the world. However, the moment they feel frightened or threatened, they return to the mindset of the traumatized child. They throw up defenses that are no longer necessary against threats that are no longer real. Maturation, however, is a journey, not a race. There's no finish line, no point at which we have learned everything we need to know, no peak of emotional health to surmount. No matter where you are in your journey, no matter how deep the wounds to your Inner Child, the techniques in this book will help you to heal through your trauma to become a resilient, nurturing parent to your Inner Self.

The Healing Inner Child process is a journey that you will continue to learn and grow throughout your life. As your awareness increases, you are more likely to see how the negative patterns of behavior that are rooted in your past are affecting your current relationships, your children, and your life. You have learned to be a better parent to your Inner Child, and you now know how to nurture an Inner Child that is ready to flourish. The Inner Child is a complete person, living in your body and mind as an individual who has a unique history of experiences and emotions. The wounded inner child is seeking love, safety, connection, and belonging. The healthy inner child, however, is seeking balance and wholeness.

A key to healing trauma and reclaiming your Inner Child is to first recognize what has happened to you as a child and the way you were treated as a child. You must first identify the hurtful and self-destructive patterns and behaviors that stem from past experiences. Your inner world will be filled with events and people that take you back through time to those painful moments, days, or years. Remember, once you have identified and acknowledged your inner wounds and negative patterns of thinking and behavior, it's time for you to connect with your Inner Child. This connection begins with understanding how we learn love. Our inner child is our first love experience, the love we learned from our caregivers in the womb. As infants and children, we learn about love and care from our primary caregivers. If we experience them as loving and reliable, we learn to trust and value ourselves and others. The opposite is also true; if we experience our primary caregivers as unreliable or uncaring, we can learn to mistrust ourselves and others, which can result in inner conflicts. This lack of trust can manifest itself in behaviors that are destructive to us later on in life.

The next step is to continue to embrace and live life to the fullest, and to maintain a healthy balance between your inner child and your responsibilities as an adult. Imagine being able to enjoy the advantages of both worlds; your inner child will let your imagination soar and enable you to think outside the box, while your adult self will know how to plan ahead and keep things organized. Continue to nurture both aspects of yourself. By doing so, you will really be able to experience the world in a much better way.

Our inner child does not exist as a separate entity from the rest of us. The inner child lives as part of an integrated personality. When we start to focus on our Inner Child, we can feel it "grow up" and begin to take on more and more adult responsibilities. During the process, we may need to release our adult mind and let go of things that we never needed anyway. We may find ourselves doing things we did not think we could and making decisions and choices we would never have made before. We may feel like we are losing ourselves, but we should recognize that what is really happening is that we are gaining a whole new way of being in the world. We may see that what used to feel like "who I am" is changing into "who I was capable of being." We may be surprised to find out who we want to be. We may start to feel that our childhood passions are returning. In the long run, we may find that we have been put on a different path, one that allows us to be at our best as adults.

At the beginning of this healing process, your relationship with your Inner Child will probably be challenging and will lead to feelings of failure and even rage against your inner self. However, as you work through these feelings and begin to live life with a higher level of awareness, it will become easier and easier for you to connect with your Inner Child. As it does, you will begin to learn how to do things for your Inner Child. This is the time when you will learn what is appropriate for your Inner Child and what is appropriate for your inner adult self. You will also begin to recognize how your emotions are showing up in the form of behavior that used to be inappropriate for you as an adult. Your Inner Child can express emotions that are triggered by present situations, but these feelings may seem inappropriate to the child.

As observed, understanding the concept of the inner child is not too complicated. With this guide, you now have a chance to improve your life. Start treating your inner child now, then see how it changes your perception and vision in life. A process of self-healing for the inner child begins with an understanding that we are shaped, in part, by our parents and by those who raised us. We may be carrying what we perceive as the pain and trauma of those early years into our current lives as adults to such a degree that we can't function as well as we want to. Psychologists spend a good deal of time trying to untangle these problems and resolve them for their patients. We can do it too. There are steps that will help you on your journey. The work may be hard because rewiring habits of thought *is* hard. We weren't wounded this deeply overnight. We're used to feeling hurt, feeling deep pain, and used to suffering. This book shares the path that has helped many people. Many people couldn't make the advice stick and couldn't permanently heal the wound. The key is facing the feeling. It requires you to express the feelings without continuing to think in the ways that fuel and feed the pain.

As a general rule, the Inner Child concept is used to explain people's inability to integrate their present self with their past self. Until a person can heal from the wounds of his or her past, they cannot be at peace with their present self. It is as if one part of them cannot be fully integrated with another. There are many factors that may contribute to a person's inability to heal from the wounds of their past. The history of these factors cannot be changed later in life.

However, the present self can learn ways to cope with the pain of the past. This can be done by empowering the Inner Child. This may sound easy, but it actually takes hard work and willingness to challenge behaviors that have been reinforced over many years. At first, you may be feeling confused about your Inner Child because your previous ideas about your past are now being questioned. That's a normal reaction. As you go through the healing process, you may eventually accept that you were the victim of abuse. If this is your experience, then you will learn how to react differently to your Inner Child. This process will be much easier, if you find someone who shares your experience and can help guide you through it. There are many online forums where you can discuss what happened with others like yourself and get support. You can also find a therapist whose practice focuses on the subject of the inner child.

There are a wide variety of techniques that can help a person recover from the betrayal and neglect they experienced as children. However, most of them focus on releasing the painful emotions from their past. The Inner Child concept offers a different approach because it helps you understand how to change behaviors, so that your Inner Child will not continue to be hurt in similar situations. When you deal with your emotions, you are actually working to change the automatic pilot response that protects your present self. You can do this by understanding how this response has worked to help you survive abuse and neglect in the past. By using this approach, you become more at peace with yourself, regardless of what happened in your past. The information contained within these pages is non-fictional and is presented as a guide to help you, the reader, identify your inner child and heal. The Inner Child is a critical part of a person's psyche. He or she is the part that makes us human. He or she is the one that makes us vulnerable, imaginative, resilient, daring, and spontaneous.

While it may seem impossible now, just remember the words of Dr. Martin Luther King, Jr.: "Take the first step in faith. You don't have to see the whole staircase, just take the first step."

Start Healing!

REFERENCES

Anderson, T. J. (2018). The Art of Health Hacking: A Personal Guide to Elevate Your State of Health and Performance, Stress Less, and Build Healthy Habits that Matter. Morgan James Publishing.

Barnard, L. K., & Curry, J. F. (2011). Self-compassion: Conceptualizations, correlates, & interventions. Review of general psychology, 15(4), 289-303.

Bradshaw, J. (2013). Homecoming: Reclaiming and Healing your Inner Child Bantam.

Brooks, J. B. (1981). The process of parenting.

Capacchione, L. (1991). Recovery of your inner child: The highly acclaimed method for liberating your inner self. Simon and Schuster.

Carr, S. M., & Hancock, S. (2017). Healing the inner child through portrait therapy: Illness, identity and childhood trauma. International Journal of Art Therapy, 22(1), 8-21.

Cates & Melinda, (2019). I Make a Difference, Melinda Cates LTD.

Dulewicz, V., & Higgs, M. (2004). Can emotional intelligence be developed? The International Journal of Human Resource Management, 15(1), 95-111.

Dzwonkowska, I., & Żak-Łykus, A. (2015). Self-compassion and social functioning of people–research review. Polish Psychological Bulletin, 46(1), 82-87.

Hanh, T. N. (2010). Reconciliation: Healing the inner child. Parallax Press.

Hanh, Thich (Oct 9, 2006 31-32), Reconciliation: Healing the Inner Child. Parallax Press,

Hubbard, P., Eagle, A. M. E., & AMFT, A. Hakomi: Working with the Inner Child, Part 2.

Ioannidou, F., & Konstantikaki, V. (2008). Empathy and emotional intelligence: What is it really about?. International Journal of caring sciences, 1(3), 118.

Ivy, M. (1996). Chapter Two Have You Seen Me? Recovering the Inner Child in Late Twentieth-Century America. In Children and the Politics of Culture (pp. 79-104). Princeton University Press.

Lantieri, L. (2008). Nurturing inner calm in children. Encounter, 21(3), 32-37.

Lerner, R. (1990). Affirmations for the inner child. Health Communications, Inc.

Lerner, R. (2010). Affirmations for the Inner Child. Simon and Schuster.

Lomas, J., Stough, C., Hansen, K., & Downey, L. A. (2012). Brief report: Emotional intelligence, victimisation and bullying in adolescents. Journal of adolescence, 35(1), 207-211.

Maunz & Ellen (2012) Nurturing Your Child's Inner Life, CreateSpace Independent Publishing Platform.

Minullina, A. (2018) Psychological Trauma of Children of Dysfunctional Families.65-74. 10.15405/epsbs.2018.09.8.

Narvaez, Darcia & Gray, Peter & McKenna, James & Fuentes, Agustin & Valentino, Kristin. (2014). Children's Development in Light of Evolution and Culture.

Neff, K. (2004). Self-compassion and psychological well-being. Constructivism in the human sciences, 9(2), 27.

Neff, K. (2015). The 5 myths of self-compassion. Psychotherapy Networker, 39(5).

Neff, K. D. (2011). Self-compassion, self-esteem, and well-being. Social and personality psychology compass, 5(1), 1-12.

O'Gorman, Patricia and Diaz, Philip, (2012) Healing Trauma through Self-Parenting: The Co-dependency Connection.

O'Shea Brown, G. (2021). Ego State Work and Connecting with the Inner Child. In Healing Complex Posttraumatic Stress Disorder (pp. 123-135). Springer, Cham.

Paul, M., & Chopich, E. (1990). Healing your aloneness: Finding love and wholeness through your inner child. Harpercollins Publishers Incorporated.

Pollard, J. K. (1987). Self-Parenting: The Complete Guide to Your Inner Conversations. Generic Human Studies Publishing.

Purvis, Karyn B. and Cross, David R. (2007) The Connected Child: Bringing Hope and Healing to your Adoptive Family, McGraw-Hill Education.

Rossi, A., Amore, M., Galderisi, S., Rocca, P., Bertolino, A., Aguglia, E., ... & Maj, M. (2018). The complex relationship between self-reported personal recovery and clinical recovery in schizophrenia. Schizophrenia research, 192, 108-112.

Schooler, Jayne and Smalley, Betsy Keefer, (2010) Wounded Children, Healing Homes: How Traumatized Children Impact Adoptive and Foster Families.

Senroy, P. (2008). Nourishing The Inner Child: The Sesame Approach of Drama and Movement Therapy with Teens

Recovering from Disordered Eating. The Creative Therapies and Eating Disorders, 209.

Sjöblom, M., Jacobsson, L., Öhrling, K., & Kostenius, C. (2021). From 9 to 91: health promotion through the life-course—illuminating the inner child. Health Promotion International, 36(4), 1062-1071.

Sprug & Joseph (1966) An Index to G.K. Chesterton, Washington: Catholic University of America Press.

Stein, S. J. (2009). Emotional intelligence for dummies. John Wiley & Sons.

Subramanian, S., & Raj, I. D. F. (2012). The efficacy of an intervention on healing the inner child on emotional intelligence, and adjustment among the college students. Indian journal of health and wellbeing, 3(3), 648-652.

Subramanian, S., & Raj, I. D. F. (2012). The efficacy of an intervention on healing the inner child on emotional intelligence, and adjustment among the college students. Indian journal of health and wellbeing, 3(3), 648-652.

Tsabary & Shefali (2016) The Awakened Family: A Revolution in Parenting, Viking.

Wallace & Kelly (2015) Healing the Child Within: Changing your Early Childhood Life Script, CreateSpace Independent Publishing Platform.

Wharam, J. (2017). Emotional intelligence: journey to the centre of yourself. John Hunt Publishing.

Whitfield, C. L. (1987). Healing the child within: Discovery and recovery for adult children of dysfunctional families (Recovery Classics Edition). Health Communications, Inc.

Made in the USA
Middletown, DE
13 October 2023

40762796R00137